THE FLOGGING OF SINGAPORE
The Michael Fay Affair

Asad Latif

TIMES BOOKS INTERNATIONAL
Singapore • Kuala Lumpur

© 1994 Times Editions Pte Ltd
Published by Times Books International
an imprint of Times Editions Pte Ltd
Times Centre
1 New Industrial Road
Singapore 1953

Times Subang
Lot 46, Subang Hi-Tech Industrial Park
Batu Tiga
40000 Shah Alam
Selangor Darul Ehsan
Malaysia

All rights reserved. No part of this publication may be reproduced, stored in a retrieval system, or transmitted, in any form or by any means, electronic, mechanical, photocopying, recording or otherwise, without the prior permission of the copyright holder.

Printed in Singapore

ISBN 981 204 530 9

CONTENTS

Acknowledgements 4

Preface 5

1 Public Thoughts 7

2 The Media War 23

3 Official Responses 54

4 Bilateral Bonds 72

5 Two Marines and a Diplomat 91

6 Conclusion 100

Epilogue 102

ACKNOWLEDGEMENTS

In writing this book, I have received the benefit of advice from colleagues and others. Leslie Fong and Han Fook Kwang enriched me with their insights into the issue, and Derwin Pereira, Warren Fernandez and Cherian George commented on the manuscript. Bertha Henson kindly agreed to proofread the book. Tan Kok Eng, my editor at Times Editions, tolerated my perennial revisions of the text with exemplary patience and good humour.

It goes without saying, of course, that they are not responsible for any errors that may remain.

My wife, Mala, in her long-suffering way, reheated those dinners while I tried to meet the deadline. To her this book is dedicated.

PREFACE

THE MICHAEL FAY AFFAIR is not only about an American teenager and Singapore. It is ultimately about an era of rapid global change which could lead to the emergence of an alternative, if not a challenge, to the model of social and political rights epitomized by the US. This is why the issue, in both the US and Singapore, touched not just on two penal systems but on many other fundamental factors, such as public opinion, the press and interstate relations. To its US critics, depending on who they were, Singapore stood guilty on multiple counts. To Singaporeans, the Fay case was being blown out of proportion by the American media. It was being transformed into an excuse for the flogging of the tiny state by the world's remaining superpower. Also, Singaporeans found it surprising that American editorial-writers and columnists were being so harsh on their city-state in spite of a significant degree of American public support for the caning sentence. What made that treatment harder to accept was that the two countries enjoyed close economic and military relations. What was going on?

An analysis of how the issue evolved clarifies the fundamental forces at work in and around it. The passions aroused by the episode will probably subside after a while, but the forces it brought to the fore may well impinge on Singapore's relations with the rest of the world in the coming years. For a country protective of its way of life and yet necessarily open to the world, the Fay affair holds important lessons.

CHAPTER I
PUBLIC THOUGHTS

ONE OF THE SURPRISES of the Fay affair was the support which the caning sentence received in the US. Mainstream America is thought of as a liberal society in which public opinion is repulsed by harsh penal measures, especially if, by inflicting pain, they fall foul of the constitutional injunction against "cruel and unusual" punishment.

At another level, many Americans are suspicious of deterrent punishment, which not only reflects the severity of the crime committed, but is meted out to deter the criminal, and others, from crime. Those opposed to it think that a person should be punished only for the crime he has committed, not to prevent him from committing it again. Similarly, since he is not responsible for what others might do, he should not be "made an example of" to deter them.

In this context, there is a widespread perception of the *rotan* as a deterrent that has helped keep Singapore relatively crime-free. The American supporters of his caning must therefore have acknowledged that they were supporting a system that believes in deterrent sentences. Such a system goes against the penal assumptions of a liberal society that generally emphasizes rehabilitation over retribution. When the crime is a nonviolent one, the need to inflict physical pain must appear even less compelling in such a society.

Why, then, did so many Americans support caning? Indeed, why did some of them go so far as to say that the US should import the sentence from Singapore?

Editorial-writers and columnists in what might be called the liberal American media argued that supporters of caning did not know what it entailed. They confused judicial caning with the paddling that many American fathers delivered to recalcitrant sons till recently. Caning — or "flogging", or "thrashing" as the sentence on Fay was described — was a form of mutilation so painful that the victim often went into shock and was unable to sit or lie on his back for days, some writers said. It left permanent physical and emotional scars. It was carried out, allegedly, by trained martial law experts, and if the victim passed out while being struck, he was revived by the prison doctor — so that the caning could go forward.

In the case of Fay, who suffered from Attention Deficit Disorder, which caused concentration and certain other problems, caning could actually make him suicidal, some suggested. Could decent, civilized Americans ever want this kind of punishment to be carried out on anyone, especially a fellow-citizen?

As Richard Cohen, a columnist for *The Washington Post,* put it, instead of Americans "protesting the flogging of one of their own", they were endorsing a cruel and unusual punishment. It was especially cruel for Fay, Cohen added, because he appeared to have been "abandoned by his own countrymen". *The New York Times* columnist William Safire similarly chided Americans who "thoughtlessly espouse torture", and an editorial in the paper said that Fay's "American detractors are simply helping Singapore score propaganda points".

The point was misdirected. Americans, both those who supported the caning and those who opposed it, had taken an interest in the case precisely because of widespread media publicity, in which the severity of the sentence had been a key factor. Some columnists and television shows had gone to remarkable lengths to show how terrible it was. It was wrong to argue, therefore, that American supporters of Singapore's stand were ignorant of what caning actually meant.

Unlike awareness of the severity of caning, the degree of support it received in America is more difficult to gauge. First, public opinion changes. Secondly, it is a fact that only those who felt strongly enough about the issue — whether they agreed or disagreed with the caning — bothered to write to the newspapers or call television talk shows to make their opinions known. The vast majority of Americans did not, and so it is not possible to know what they thought.

That notwithstanding, the Fay issue revealed an unexpected depth of public support for tough punishments among Americans. A Singapore Embassy official in Washington was quoted in early April 1994 as having said that it had received more than 100 letters and 200 telephone calls in recent weeks, with the vast majority expressing "very strong support" for Singapore. Many of the letters said that the US would have far less crime if punishments were harsher.

In the press, *Chicago Tribune* columnist Mike Royko, who wrote on the Fay affair, said that he had received scores of letters from readers, with 99 per cent arguing that Fay should be caned. Some Americans even wrote to *The Straits Times* saying that the punishment should go ahead.

As for television, it was revealed that 70 per cent of American viewers who had taken part in a telephone poll in March 1994 supported caning. However, a telephone poll of 751 adults carried out by *Newsweek* in April showed that 52 per cent of Americans disapproved of it.

The two trends ran neck and neck in a *Los Angeles Times* survey that interviewed 1,682 adults from 16 to 19 April; 49 per cent supported the sentence and 48 per cent disapproved of it. Interestingly, however, of the 2,270 people who called the *Dayton Daily News*, in Fay's hometown of Dayton in Ohio, for a phone-in poll, 1,442 approved of the caning, while 828 did not.

Clarence Page, a nationally-syndicated columnist, found it significant that public support for caning was overwhelming in Dayton.

"What Dayton thinks is particularly significant," he wrote in a column published by the *Washington Times*, "because Dayton has long been viewed by marketing experts and political pollsters as a bellwether for the nation.

"Companies test the appeal of their products with Dayton consumers. Political pundits and consultants parachute into Dayton every four years to test Middle American political views. As Dayton goes, so goes America."

One reason for the interest in Fay was that his caning sentence coincided with a renewed debate on crime and punishment in America. In fact, the House of Representatives passed a Bill in April that includes a mandatory life sentence after three convictions for violent crime. The Bill also adds to the statute books dozens of crimes punishable by death.

Nevertheless, Americans were tired of the disproportionality between punishment and crime in their penal system, which was geared heavily towards treating the criminal as a person victimized by society and hence deserving of its understanding. That was the thrust of its rehabilitative approach, which weighed more heavily than a punitive one, where the criminal paid a personal price for his crimes instead of dumping them on society and "root causes" — deprivation, poverty, alienation, hopelessness.

That is why Americans were applauding Singapore, where punishment was being meted out swiftly. Law-abiding American citizens were exasperated with their society's liberal, rehabilitative approach to crime, whose result, many think, has been to give criminals an easy ride while the victims of crime have nowhere to turn to. The caning sentence brought to the surface a strong current of popular dissatisfaction with the US legal system.

To say this is not to dismiss — as Fay's supporters in the media did — support for caning as the readiness of unfeeling Americans to accept the alleged brutalization of one of their own in a distant land merely because they were dissatisfied with their own judicial system. The truth might be that Middle America is far more conservative than is imagined abroad. Maybe people yearn for far more than is understood — for the America of an earlier period, when families were less prone to break up, parents were obeyed, the education system was less prone to the vagaries of experiments and the constraints of Political Correctness, the streets were safer and society was a lot more cohesive.

That America existed as late as in the 1950s, and it resembled today's Singapore. Perhaps the support for caning revealed a deep nostalgia for those times; to the extent which Singapore reminded Americans of those times, they supported its penal system, even though it affected one of their own.

Fay's defenders will no doubt answer that *that* America got by fine without judicial caning. They have a point. It is incontrovertible that tough — or what they would call harsh — punishments are not the only guarantee against crime; indeed, they might not guarantee less crime at all. What is required is that punishments be predictable and swift, and even these punishments cannot exist in a social vacuum. Society must give the individual a sufficient economic and moral stake in order to act as a true deterrent to crime.

Some Americans opposed to Fay's sentence argued

that Singapore's relatively crime-free society was as much a result of its strong family unit, good schooling and full employment as of its penal system. As one writer asked, extending the argument, why was it that the Scandinavian countries, which coddled criminals with social care, had lower crime rates than a certain South American country where poor street-children suspected of theft were shot by guards hired by businessmen, with the bodies left on the street as a message to other street-children?

In other words, while American supporters of caning demanded deterrent laws as an answer to their woes over crime, some of those opposed to corporal punishments (and other tough/harsh laws) argued that punishments do not work without an entire network of social institutions that reduce the individual's need to commit a crime.

The first group fell roughly into the category of "conservatives", the second into those of "liberals". Conservatives generally emphasize the functional. They ask whether something works in a given situation, and if it does, it is a justifiable basis of policy, whether economic, political, social or judicial. Liberals, on the other hand, do not dismiss functionality but may probe more deeply the probable costs of a functional solution in terms of fairness and equity.

Both approaches are legitimate; both need to be balanced in a society that desires both fairness and order. Where exactly that balance will be struck depends on how citizens view their society. Do they find the existing state of affairs acceptable? That is, do they think that there is an effective balance between fairness and order? Or do they think that society leans more to the side of one against the other?

The Fay affair showed that many Americans, responding to the liberal framework within which sentencing policy operates in the US, believed that their society leans too far on the side of lenience.

Even President Clinton, who criticized the sentence on Fay as excessive, acknowledged at an MTV forum with young Americans on 19 April 1994 that societies could go to the extreme, either in the direction of individual rights or in that of group rights. Part of the reason why many Asian societies had low crime rates and high economic growth rates was that these were coherent societies "where the unit is more important than the individual — whether it's the family unit or the work unit or the community unit".

Looking at America, he said that the Constitution emphasized individual rights to protect the individual from being messed around by the government — which was once a real problem — but it was assumed that Americans would use their rights responsibly. By contrast, in today's America, there was a lot of irresponsibility. Some people complained that there was too much personal freedom.

"When personal freedom is being abused, you have to move to limit it," the President said.

This was by no means an endorsement of the Singapore view, but it offered an interesting perspective on the debate on crime and punishment in the US — by the most powerful person in the country.

***

The Research and Information Department of the Singapore Press Holdings carried out a comprehensive survey of public opinion on the Fay affair whose results were released in May 1994. It covered adult Singaporean citizens and permanent residents, with a quota sample of 705 respondents selected so that they represented the general population in terms of sex, race, age, type of housing they lived in and educational qualifications.

The results revealed both the extent and the depth of public support for caning for vandalism. Overall, 87 per cent of Singaporeans favoured it. Then, there was a notable confluence of opinion within each category. Finally, there was close correspondence between the categories. Thus, 90 per cent of males and 83 per cent of females supported caning, as did 87 per cent of Chinese and 85 per cent of non-Chinese. Eighty-two per cent of one to three-roomed HDB dwellers were in its favour, as were 88 per cent of four to five-roomed HDB dwellers and 93 per cent in private housing. Among those aged between 15 and 29, the support rate was 86 per cent; for those aged 30-44, it was 85 per cent; while for those over 45, it was 90 per cent. Going by educational attainments, 84 per cent of those with less than an O-Level wanted vandals caned, while 88 per cent of those with O-Levels or higher degrees wanted the same.

The survey also gauged Singaporeans' awareness of the Fay case and their views on how safe the country was.

While it was obvious that an overwhelming majority supported caning, the survey — which was carried out on the basis of telephone interviews, with fieldwork being conducted on 4 to 5 May 1994 — did not distinguish between responses to the caning sentence itself and reactions to President Clinton's intervention and other pressures on the government, which influenced their perceptions of the issue.

There is an important qualitative point here. The issue of caning engaged Singaporeans; the issue of intervention strengthened that sense of engagement. While the degree of support for caning was high in any case, what cemented it was displeasure at being pressured by a foreign government. That conclusion is justified if we sample responses to Fay's sentence before, and after, the US media, some Senators and ultimately President Clinton got involved.

The difference was suggested in a letter to *The Straits Times* by Gopal Baratham. "It is outrageous for the American Embassy or anybody else to interfere in the Michael Fay case...Singaporeans should, however, reflect on whether caning for nonviolent crimes is compatible with our aspirations to build a humane, caring society. Are things more precious than human flesh?"

In the early months of the Fay affair, Singaporeans generally supported caning, though some counselled lenience. One said that Singapore should be gracious and just deport Fay. Another said that he, like other Singaporeans, was being driven by contradictory feelings. "We say... "ya, ya, he deserves it...but deep inside wonder about the direction of punishment-versus-crime here."

Yeong Ah Seng, who edits *The Straits Times'* Forum page, says that out of the 600 or so letters he had received on the Fay issue — 400 before the caning and 200 after it — about 90 per cent were in favour of the punishment. Significantly, however, 25 per cent of the letters came from foreigners resident in Singapore and Americans and others abroad, and these were overwhelmingly in favour of the caning, while the few expressions of sympathy Fay received came largely from Singaporeans.

This appears to suggest that Singaporeans, beneficiaries of a penal system that made them feel secure, were more likely to be sympathetic to a young offender than Americans at the receiving end of their society's approach to crime.

One point that did not draw much attention was the irony seemingly at work in the issue. The US, reputed to be the most individualistic country on earth, was asking society to take responsibility for the individual's actions. And then there was communitarian Singapore saying that individuals were responsible for what they did.

But the irony was only an apparent one. By emphasizing that society was a co-bearer of the individual's burden, the US was allowing its criminals to get away with light sentences. In this sense, it was defending their individuality. By refusing to have society bear responsibility for the individual's actions, Singapore was pushing back responsibility to the individual, upholding the interests of society. Its punishments reflected individual, not social, responsibility. Their toughness and predictability followed from this.

A great number of Singaporeans supported that approach. This was evident from their immediate response to the news in October 1993 that a group of teenage foreigners had been taken in by the police in connection with a spate of acts of vandalism.

In a report on 8 October 1993 headlined "Vandalism spree provokes outraged reaction from public", *The Straits Times* said businessman Joseph Wong had called it to say that the students should be punished severely. "Such social behaviour should not be imported into our country."

A 19-year-old student, Tan Geok Mei, said: "As guests staying here, they should observe the law and not tarnish the image of their own countries."

Indeed, according to the Commander of Tanglin Police Station, Superintendent Lum Hon Fye, several people had called the police about the vandalism. The callers evidently felt that the suspects might get off lightly because they were foreigners, for he assured people that the police were viewing the matter very seriously. "The suspects may be foreigners from well-to-do families but they will not get any preferential treatment. The police will treat them like any Singaporean offender," he said.

Indeed, one interesting aspect of the affair was whether Singaporeans were asking for a tough stance on the alleged vandals because they were foreigners, or whether they wanted tough action in spite of the fact that they were foreigners.

Derek Ee Ming Chong seemed to imply the former when he wrote: "It seems odd that when local teenage vandals strike, very seldom do we find Singaporeans reacting so vehemently.

"Yes, vandalism whether by foreign students or Singaporeans, is wrong. But that does not warrant such harsh treatment and punishment, especially in a civilized city-state like Singapore. They should be warned, counselled and fined heavily."

Others implied the latter.

More significant than this difference, however, was the difference between the responses of Singaporeans to the caning sentence itself and their anger over US attempts to have it revoked. Nationalist sentiments were in rich evidence among those who wrote to the press to comment on the US pressure. No matter what many Singaporeans thought about caning — and, as we have seen, there were voices pleading against it — they were united in their opposition to pressure from abroad. Indeed, caning as an issue became entirely subservient to the pressure as an issue.

Thus, Tin Keng Seng argued in a letter published on 8 April 1994 that apart from the law, which stipulated caning for vandalism, there were reasons why

President Ong Teng Cheong should turn down appeals for Fay's clemency made by 24 US Senators. First, it would "send a wrong signal to other foreigners residing in Singapore that they can flout the law and resort to diplomatic or political channels to escape punishment".

Secondly, revoking the sentence would "smack of double standards and Singaporeans would soon question the rule of law here". Thirdly, if Singapore succumbed to foreign intervention in the administration of justice, "what would that imply for the sovereignty of the nation?"

Those who were "lobbying to undermine the law in Singapore", he said, were trying to turn it into a political issue and signal to Singaporeans that might makes right.

The issue of sovereignty was also the theme of a letter by Ng Chong Jin, who argued that the Americans "are trying to browbeat and pressure us politically... It is incredible that Americans never seem to learn that political arm-twisting and loud gestures do not work on everyone."

Given the strength of public support for resisting US pressure, it was natural that some Singaporeans responded with disappointment, if not anger, to the government's decision to reduce the sentence from six strokes to four.

While it was undeniably true that the government had upheld a crucial point of principle — the right of Singapore to cane vandals, whether local or foreign, under its laws — even the reduction in the sentence was seen as a step back in the face of US pressure.

In a long letter on 6 May 1994 drawing attention to the fact that earlier statements by political leaders and government officials had defended the sentence and ruled out any compromise, Singapore political scientist Hussin Mutalib remarked: "What is at issue here is not simply the caning of Michael Fay, but whether or not a state, any state, is allowed to exercise its own laws in its own way."

He asked what would happen if, in the future, other countries were to appeal on behalf of their citizens for offences they had committed in Singapore.

In another letter, Cheang Wai Yew expressed his "disbelief" over the reduction in the sentence and said that the reason given for it — that the gesture would go some way to meeting President Clinton's concern — was "ludicrous". "He might even laugh at our halfhearted resolution."

Tan Peng Choo, a businessman, was forthright. "Our ties with the US should have no bearing on the issue here, which is a question of law," he said. B. Devi, a businesswoman, asked if the government would have made an exception for an offender from the Third World. A grassroots leader expressed shock at the reduction, especially since it "does not satisfy America, and it does not please Singaporeans either".

A *Straits Times* straw poll revealed that 22 people out of 40 academics, community leaders, professionals and Members of Parliament had supported the reduction in the sentence. They believed that it would not set a precedent and, as the managing director of an accounting firm noted, "showing compassion is not a bad idea. And it is also helpful to maintain good relations with an ally".

***

American and Singaporean public opinion, to the extent it could be gauged, was closer over the Fay issue than would be suspected given impressions of a massive cultural divide between the two countries. Mainstream opinion in both countries was shown to be conservative. While this does not necessarily mean that a majority of Americans would want to adopt Singapore's penal system wholesale, it is apparent that there is in the US a genuine streak of conservative opposition to its liberal ethos, of which penology is a part. In Singapore, few would want to import that ethos and have it translated into laws, but this did not prevent some Singaporeans from responding to Fay as a person and asking for compassion on humanitarian grounds. However, once President Clinton had intervened publicly on his behalf, there was a strong feeling in Singapore that the integrity of its judicial system needed to be upheld. That sentiment overshadowed whatever sympathy there was for Fay.

The US media played a critical role in turning Fay into an issue between the two governments. The Singapore media, too, influenced opinions on the affair. To that media war we now turn.

CHAPTER II
THE MEDIA WAR

HUMAN BEINGS, the sociologist Charles Wright Mills once remarked, live in second-hand worlds. These are networks of "observation posts", "interpretation centres" and "presentation depots". Together, they make up what he called the cultural apparatus.*

The cultural apparatus being *par excellence* one of communication, the media is an intrinsic part of it. Drawing from an inexorable and inchoate flow of occurrences in society, the media selects, filters, imbues with meaning and attaches value to certain events, which it then communicates as "news". Words on the page, sounds on the air and images on the television screen communicate to the audience nothing less than a view of the world and a sense of its place in it. The words and characters grow into themes, patterns and ideologies, legitimizing, supporting and reinforcing each other. The media not only tells people what they ought to know, but also what they ought to believe.

This does not mean that readers agree with or believe all that they read or see: they may well disagree and disbelieve. However, whether they agree or disagree,

---

* "Power, Politics and People", in *The Collected Essays of C. Wright Mills,* ed. Irving Louis Horowitz, Oxford University Press, London, Oxford, New York, 1967.

believe or disbelieve, the important thing is that they agree or disagree with what they read or see. Their response to events and issues of the day is shaped to a large extent by what appears in print or on the screen. News is not what happens — for so much happens that goes unreported — but is what editors and reporters judge to be sufficiently important to bring to their readers' notice. By the very act of deciding what is news, newspeople daily reinforce readers' expectation of what constitutes news. Newspapers also provide the parameters for readers' responses: they set an agenda. There is nothing necessarily sinister about this. All newspapers around the world do it, though what agenda they set naturally differs from country to country and system to system.

The American media is not a monolith; it prides itself on its diversity as on its independence. Like the media in any advanced democracy, it is indeed diverse, stretching from the grand national dailies — *The New York Times, The Washington Post, The Los Angeles Times, The Christian Science Monitor, USA Today* and so on — to small town and community papers, to say nothing of the sensationalist tabloids. These papers differ in their political affiliations — they cover the entire spectrum from the liberal to the arch-conservative — as much as they do in their circulation and budgets. To that must be added the perhaps even wider scope of a multitude of radio and television stations, whose package of entertainment, news, current-affairs programmes and talk shows reaches into every nook and cranny of America.

For all its diversity, however, the US media is nationalistic, most of all when it comes to protecting what it considers national values from a foreign "onslaught". That explains why the fortunes of a single American abroad became the subject of such consuming media interest, not only in news columns but in a veritable deluge of columns and editorials that opposed his punishment in almost millennial terms.

Nationalism also explains why this happened though Singapore, the object of their ire, was not only not an enemy of the US but actually one of its closest partners in Asia.

And, interestingly, nationalism suggests why the media justified its stance on the issue when it ran directly counter to that part of US public opinion which not only supported Fay's sentence but would have it imported to America.

In his seminal study of the US media, Herbert J. Gans observes that, in common with the media of other countries, "American foreign news is ultimately only a variation on domestic themes". The media's interpretations apply American values. It may not follow US foreign policy slavishly, but it is "closer to the State Department line on foreign news than to the White House line on domestic news".*

However, while there is much in common between

---

* *Deciding What's News. A Study of "CBS Evening News", "NBC Nightly News", Newsweek and Time,* Vintage Books, New York, 1980, pp. 37-38.

US media and media elsewhere, there is something that distinguishes American journalism from that elsewhere, including the rest of the West. This, says the cultural critic Edward Said, is the knowledge among American journalists that their country is a superpower "with interests and ways of pursuing those interests" which other countries do not possess. Moreover, US journalists belong to media organizations that view themselves as participants in the power of the American state. When that power is threatened, the media, for all the space it genuinely provides to a diversity of views, falls back on defending and reiterating the nationalist consensus, expressed in a corporate identity called "America" or even "the West".

In its domestic coverage, the media tries to recast the great diversity of multicultural America in terms of this nationalist consensus. Following the same logic, it tries to recast the diversity of the rest of the world "in a uniquely American way".*

This is an important point. The media is a cultural product. Its reflexes and responses are shaped by the culture it is part of. In responding to a different culture, the media tries to recreate it in the image of its own culture. The media anywhere does this. What is special about the US media is that the culture which has produced it is dominant in the world. Dominance confers on the US media the power to claim that its

---

* *Covering Islam: How The Media And The Experts Determine How We View The Rest Of the World,* Routledge and Kegan Paul, London, Melbourne and Henley, 1981, pp. 47-49.

recreation of reality is the most legitimate one, if not the sole one.

This recasting of reality is not limited to the media, of course. It can be seen in academia, where scholars subject other cultures to the terms of reference applicable to their own cultures, recreating reality in their own image. This is especially so with scholars in the West, who belong to a historical tradition of intellectual dominance growing out of the West's early start in industrialization and the history of colonialism. The re-creation of Oriental reality by the Occident was the subject of Said's *tour de force, Orientalism.**

To mention Said is not to suggest that the American state "adopted" Fay as a nationalist cause, "activated" its ties with the corporate media and turned him over to it so that it could build a nationalist consensus around him. Apart from misrepresenting Said's approach, that would be wrong. What interest could the mighty political and diplomatic machine called Washington, D.C., have in an 18-year-old charged with vandalism in Singapore? He had not even committed a "political" offence. What, then, could there be in the issue for the US government to exploit?

Indeed not. It was the other way around. In its attempt to create a nationalist consensus on the Fay issue, the media, acting as a collection of corporate bodies which view themselves as sharing in the power of the American state, was responding as an autonomous collection of media entities, but a collection

---

* Penguin Books, Middlesex, 1985.

responding nevertheless to what it saw as a challenge to the power of the American state.

Where did that challenge come from? It came from a shift in the international balance of economic (and hence political) power in which culture is an important element. The American state had a major interest in how the shift turned out. Fay involuntarily became an issue in those magisterial affairs.

What was happening was this. US relations with almost all Asian countries are undergoing a process of readjustment following the end of the Cold War, the disappearance of the Soviet threat and the emergence of Asian centres of power, principally China. During the Cold War, Washington mediated among Asian countries united in their opposition to the Soviet Union. The US was not only an Asian power but was the leader of an informal Asian alliance.

With the disappearance of the Soviet threat, the US became the world's remaining superpower, but ironically, its very preeminence was accompanied by a dramatic change in its relations with its Asian friends. With different motivations and in differing degrees, Asian countries began seeking a new relationship with the US, a new deal closer to their own terms, which were no longer tied to the past partnership directed against the Soviet Union. In this new deal, they wanted recognition of the fact that the world's economic centre of gravity was moving towards Asia as the Pacific Century dawned.

Of course the US was a Pacific power; indeed, its

cooperation was vital to secure the success of the Pacific Century. It was not that the US was falling behind, but that others were catching up. However, the point remained: the new deal would have to be one between equals, reflecting the growing clout of Asia.

And it is here that the cultural element came in. East Asian leaders have become vocal in pointing out the cultural bases of the boom that has transformed the region. They argue that values such as strong familial ties, hard work, thrift and communitarianism account for the social cohesion that enables high growth rates to be achieved. The West was on the ascendant when it possessed these values; its degeneration into libertarianism and welfarism explains its current economic woes.

Attitudes to crime and punishment are intrinsic to cultural differences between the East and the West. The latter, it is argued, has gone soft on crime, leading to soaring crime rates. The situation has been worsened by a tendency to explain criminal behaviour in terms of a variety of syndromes and take a lenient view of criminals because they are the product of "root causes" such as poverty, deprivation and alienation.

In the East, by contrast, individuals, not society and root causes, are held responsible for their actions. Criminals are not dealt with leniently because they allegedly suffer from syndromes. Indeed, deterrent sentences are handed down to keep society relatively crime-free.

On all these fronts, the US, and the West generally,

have come under criticism from emergent Asian systems, which claim that they are better than decadent systems in the West.

The US media's response to the Fay case was at heart a response to these criticisms. The media turned him into an innocent American abroad, an "ordinary" guy, being victimized in a culturally alien system. Fay became a symbol of the helplessness of America, and hence American values, in a world where not only were other systems on the ascendant, but where they dared to punish an American on their own terms — and, by implication, reject the values of the system that had produced Fay.

The caning of Fay sublimated the insecurities facing America as it witnessed the international challenges thrust upon it. Like vicarious pleasure, there is vicarious pain. The very mental image of an American being caned became a challenge to the self-image of America as its media pictured it.

And here, to return to Said's point, the media of the superpower behaved as it has behaved. It turned its ideological guns on "upstart" Singapore, a country that had challenged its self-image and was expressing the self-confidence of an alternative cultural system on the ascendant.

The New York Times led the charge for the liberals in its editorials. The first one condemned Singapore's "repellent sense of justice", which could hand down a "grossly disproportionate" sentence "akin to torture".

An editorial on 10 April 1994 went further. Referring,

no doubt, to those Americans who were flooding the Singapore Embassy in Washington with calls in support of the caning, it said that Fay's "American detractors" were "helping Singapore score propaganda points". It asked those opposed to the punishment to call the embassy, whose number it provided, and mentioned a number of American corporations that did business in Singapore, asking them to lean on the authorities.

Three days later, an even sharper editorial followed. It gave the names, not only of companies, but of their CEOs, doing business in Singapore. Arguing that "Singapore needs such people as friends," it directed them to make their voices heard. The Fay issue, it thought, gave Americans a legitimate reason to use political and economic pressure to propagate freedom and basic rights.

The Christian Science Monitor saw Fay as a victim of the ongoing debate over Asian and Western values, a debate that touches on penology, different value-systems and diverging norms of civil and political rights.

Its editorial of 8 April said it was not accidental that the "defiant Asian lobby" at the United Nations Conference on Human Rights in Vienna in June 1993 had been led by Mr Lee Kuan Yew. That "lobby" had demanded that human rights be based on cultural norms, not universal values.

The sentence on Fay "did not just happen", the paper declared. "It is an object lesson for the West, whose culture Mr Lee and other Islamic (or Confucian) leaders feel is lost in a degenerating moral nihilism. It is not going too far to say that the caning of Fay is an almost literal expression of what Samuel Huntington has called an emerging 'clash of civilizations'."

Bob Deans, writing for Cox News Service from Singapore, saw the issue as capturing "a new mood of assertiveness" in East Asian countries. For nearly half a decade, the US military umbrella had protected the region while American investment and trade had benefited it.

That prosperity had created "mounting confidence and psychological independence" from Seoul to Singapore. The lights were dimming on an era when the US called all the shots with its partners in East Asia.

"That the stage for ushering out that age winds up being tiny Singapore only makes the irony that much richer," Deans concluded.

The cultural point merged into an ethnic one in some comments. Since East Asia, influenced by the Confucianist cultures of China and Japan, was at the heart of the new challenge to America, surely the sentence on Fay must reflect Singapore's connection with the Confucianist tradition and the supposed links of its majority community with an assertive China.

In a column in *The Washington Post* on 22 March, Jim Hoagland argued that the Fay issue revealed attitudes of cultural supremacy among many Asians, particularly Chinese, towards foreigners, especially Americans. The Fay sentence was partly a "knee-jerk reflex" by a Chinese minority — no doubt a reference to Chinese Singaporeans' position in Southeast Asia — that viewed itself as "surrounded by a hostile Muslim population" and which was responding to a "culturally inferior" West on which it nevertheless depended.

As China regained its "great power complex", the Han disdain for neighbours "now extends further".

Fay, Hoagland thought, would have to pay the price for wandering into "the path of a lot of history".

(Singapore's Ambassador to the US, Mr S.R. Nathan, responded in a letter to the *International Herald Tribune*, which had reprinted Hoagland's column. He noted that caning had been introduced into Singapore not by the Chinese, but by the British colonial government. Most of those caned had been Asians. Malaysia, which was predominantly Malay and Muslim, had caning on its statute books, and had even extended the punishment to white-collar crimes.)

But that was not sufficient. In order to prove the alleged victimization of Fay, it would not do to say simply that he had wandered into the path of history. It would be necessary to locate Singapore precisely on the political atlas, describe what an aberrant system it supposedly possessed and then show how Fay was a direct victim of its alien laws.

The media, anywhere in the world, works by presenting images to its audience and invoking the meanings it expects the audience to give to them. In the Fay affair, it was evidently necessary to situate Singapore in a political landscape whose geography would be immediately recognizable to Americans. The way to do that was to use the political markers Americans could identify with instinctively: democracy and human rights.

On television, this was done in various ways. One station flew a team to Singapore to file a report. It created an image of Singapore as an affluent and clean city, the price being an inflexible legal system that mandated a host of penalties and an acquiescent populace that refused to rock the political boat. A talk show allowed participants, including Mr George Fay, Fay's father, Mrs Randy Chan, his mother, and Mr Theodore Simon, his American lawyer, to make sweeping charges against Singapore's penal and judicial system. The resources of television — sight and sound — were used to their fullest in the coverage of the case.

The press did not lag behind. In a *New York Times* column on 7 April, William Safire declared that caning was the "torture of choice" of the "dictatorship of Singapore". With a single word — dictatorship — the parameters of abhorrence had been set.

Unlike the elaborate explanation that had gone into trying to equate caning with torture in the column, there was no attempt to show how Singapore was a dictatorship. But the deed was done. Since Singapore had been declared a "dictatorship", a victim of its laws automatically became a political victim.

The attack was an especially cruel one because it came from Safire, a columnist regarded highly both for his incisive commentary and for his careful choice of words. Indeed, his essays on English usage are part of a distinguished tradition. In this case, somehow, the stringent standards he imposes on himself were not apparent.

A.M. Rosenthal chipped in a few days later in the same paper. Though the thrust of his piece was to scold Americans for protesting only when one of their own was caned, and though he certified Singapore's human rights record as far better than China's, he commented that the "vicious flogging" was part of a panoply of other laws, "the whole nasty authoritarian collection".

In a *Washington Post* editorial on 11 April, the condemnation of Singapore's political system took a strange turn: towards a comparison with the ex-Soviet Union.

The paper remembered how apologists for the old Soviet system used to argue that Moscow's crime rates were lower than those of New York's or Detroit's. That was no justification for human rights abuses by the communists; equally, therefore, America's shortcomings did not justify the sentence on Fay.

With a single stroke, Singapore was dubiously put in the same political league as the now discredited Soviet system — in the hope, evidently, of tapping residual American distaste for the fallen empire. Also, it was implied, the Soviet Union had come down (and America survives) in spite of its safe streets. Singaporeans, went the message, beware.

The widely-circulated *USA Today* referred more directly to the civil liberties which Americans held dear.

Americans, it decided, were all better off in spite of

the crime rates. This was because the US Constitution prohibited cruel and unusual punishment to protect people from intimidation by the government.

"Imagine living without that protection. Imagine living in pretty, bloody Singapore."

It is not that dissenting voices were absent.

Charles Krauthammer's was one. In a column in *The Washington Post* on 8 April, he argued that America's concern with individual rights could actually be counterproductive for its democracy.

For the past 30 years, he said, America had been obsessed with "root causes" and had invested massively in fighting them. Yet the root causes were still there, and the crime rate had tripled. "In Singapore, they do not give a hoot about root causes... And they have practically wiped out crime."

The backlash to the "laissez-faire, everything-goes regime" of the past 30 years was coming.

"The best argument for a moderate retreat from the extreme libertarianism that has left our public spaces so decayed is that the alternative is full retreat: as the chaos deepens, the calls for an authoritarian solution will grow."

This is what was happening in Russia. "America is living somewhere between Singapore and Moscow," Krauthammer observed. "If we want to preserve our liberties in the long run, we would do well to take one step toward Singapore."

But voices such as his were few. Generally, the Fay issue gave the US media a free hand against Singapore.

The Media War

Accuracy in Media, Inc., a Washington, D.C.-based organization, criticized what it called lopsided reporting and unfair commentary. In a report in April 1994, it discussed two television programmes, ABC's "World News Tonight", telecast on 16 March, and the NBC magazine show, "Now", shown on 4 April, and criticized Safire for calling Singapore a "lawless" state.

"The media are saturating us with stories about the upsurge of urban crime," it noted. "Yet they shy away from acknowledging that the American public is prepared to embrace draconian measures to curb crime...if they think they will work."

***

Singapore's media, like its US counterpart, works by setting the agenda for its audience and it is nationalistic. It is not as diverse as the US media, however. More important, it is not the voice of a superpower but that of a super small-state which must accept vulnerability as a fact of life. That vulnerability includes the cultural.

Singapore-bashing in the US media was a reminder that, close bilateral relations notwithstanding, the Republic remained an alien reality to sections of American opinion. The vilification of Singapore was an attempt by a dominant culture to subdue, remould and pacify a culture it could not or would not understand. The response, as target-cultures have always responded, was to justify and reiterate the logic of the indigenous culture. It was a defensive response, but one that was understandable.

Thus, *The Straits Times* and *The Sunday Times*, for example, were essentially reactive in their coverage of the issues thrown up by the case. Editorials and columns responded to the criticism being voiced in the US and defended Singapore's right to uphold its judicial system. Rarely did they go on the offensive and castigate the US social, political and legal system in turn.

Thus, a *Straits Times* editorial on 10 March 1994 asked what should be made of the President of the United States intervening on Fay's behalf. "Incredulity would be the reaction of many a Singaporean who learns that the world's most powerful politician, upon prompting from a reporter's question in the White House last Friday, has taken a personal interest in a case which concerns neither political hostage-taking nor a breach of national security."

It agreed sarcastically that US politicians had to respond to demanding constituents. "A subject for political enjoinment can be as big or as trivial as the public chooses to make it. Singaporeans who find his intervention objectionable need to understand that heroic gestures go down well with the American public."

Though this "clearly qualifies as interference by the White House" in the affair, Singaporeans should not overreact by being defensive about the stringency of their laws, it advised.

Given the stance the paper had adopted on the issue and the depth of public disappointment over the reduction of Fay's sentence, it said on 6 May 1994 that the government should "note the disquiet".

"In wanting to meet President Bill Clinton part of the way, as the government says, it has dismayed a section of Singaporean opinion which holds that the authorities should have stuck it out as it has the commanding heights in moralism and jurisdictional rights," it argued.

"Neither could it mollify Washington and the merchants of hysteria and disinformation in the American liberal establishment, whose campaign against Singapore has been asking that the basis of its penology be scrapped as it does not conform to American values."

The editorial acknowledged that the government had upheld caning as a principle of penology and that Singapore needed to balance domestic political realities with geopolitical realities.

"Much play is made in the official statement of the good relations with the US and of its economic and security contributions to Asia-Pacific stability. To those in favour of giving the Americans some latitude, taking into account the special relationship between the two countries, the justification would make more palatable an uncharacteristic pliability," it admitted.

"But this would barely pass muster with those Singaporeans who are either incensed by the gorilla heaviness of some American media advocates whose chutzpah they see as exceeded only by their ignorance, or view the trade and diplomatic angle as irrelevant to a judicial matter."

Ultimately, this was a case of exercising political

judgment. "Time will tell if the government had acted correctly. For now it would have to take note of the unhappiness expressed by concerned Singaporeans who had backed it fully in taking the hard line, not out of jingoism but on a point of principle."

The official commitment that the reduction would not set a precedent was one which "Singaporeans will expect it to uphold — come hell or high water".

On 13 May 1994, the paper responded to news that US Trade Representative Mickey Kantor did not want the World Trade Organization's first meeting to be held in Singapore.

"If the US is the only superpower left, it needs to behave like one," its editorial said.

"If the WTO can be dragged into a bilateral squabble, just as the Olympic movement was debased over the argument about China's human rights record, a new and dangerous distortion would become the norm in the conduct of international relations. America would not want to claim the patent rights to that, surely."

As for just how badly Fay had been hurt by the caning, the extent of the injuries was irrelevant, it said. However, if the State Department did not believe the Prisons Department's account, "it should say outright that the Singapore Government is lying. The Government will no doubt respond appropriately." It called for an end to the "spectacle". "It was amusing, now it gets tiresome."

While the paper's editorials were pointed, they were restrained. Columnists, expectedly, were more forthright.

The Media War

In a column in *The Sunday Times* on 10 April 1994, Warren Fernandez wrote scathingly of the double standards evident in the US response to the case.

He noted how the US had gone ahead with the North American Free Trade Agreement with Mexico in spite of the brutal suppression of the Chiapas peasant revolt by the Mexican military in January 1993. Indeed, Mexico had been admitted to the Organization for Economic Cooperation and Development, a club for the industrial democracies.

By contrast, Washington continued to hector Beijing over its human rights record more than four years after the Tiananmen incident.

Similarly for the "American hyperbole" on the Fay issue.

Fernandez thought that the pressure being exerted on Singapore was not directed at putting an end to flogging *per se*. "What the Americans are now pushing for, however, amounts to an altogether different proposition — namely, that an American should be exempt from Singapore's tough laws because some Americans find these laws distasteful."

"Worse, that Americans should now argue that a country's laws should be applied with provisos makes a mockery of their high-minded, long-held advocacy of the rule of law, both within states and in relations between them."

This also called into question the Western belief that globalization would give rise to universally shared values.

Lamentably, instead, the US political elite was arrogating to itself the right to frame universal laws unilaterally. Some Americans went even further: they wanted America to use its economic muscle to enforce these dictates.

"But when these rules no longer suit them, do not be too surprised if they are ignored ever-so-blithely, or worse, modified summarily. After all, it would not be the first time."

Chua Huck Cheng, *The Straits Times'* chief leader-writer, criticized America's agitprop methods and its threats of "economic aggression" after it had lost the argument.

Noting the various attempts to pressure Singapore, he exclaimed: "My, aren't we raising American behinds on a pedestal! This does not even qualify as a clumsy attempt at nationalistic one-upmanship; such reasoning in this geopolitical age shows at best, ignorance of Singapore as a polity and, at worst, arrested development."

He argued that "there are few civil liberties the Americans get which are denied Singaporeans.

"Why can't the Americans be like us? But we do not impose our values on others."

In her weekly *Sunday Times* piece on 24 April, veteran columnist Tan Sai Siong approached the issue differently by drawing attention to how the torrent of abuse unleashed on the Republic might affect Singaporeans.

Some of them "may wish to make Fay a proxy for

their anger against the unfair, nay downright biased, picture that has been painted of Singapore".

However, that should not be so. In any case, "our tough laws do not need external validation".

"If Fay is spared, it is not because of fear or favour. It is because after a thorough review, mitigating factors outweigh the negative."

That said, "if the most powerful country in the world does not have the power to teach its citizens how to behave before exporting them, then it is tantamount to inviting less powerful but responsible host countries to play disciplinarian."

Following the reduction in Fay's sentence, Han Fook Kwang, Deputy Political Editor of *The Straits Times*, pondered the meaning of the government's decision on 7 May.

He admitted that the government needed to protect the system's integrity against external interference, but there was also the question of how Singapore should deal with President Clinton's repeated appeals.

The US was a major trading partner and had a stabilizing military presence in Asia. "More important, the possibility that sometime in the future, for whatever reason, Singapore might need US help should not be ruled out."

The decision, he noted, boiled down to "two strokes to limit the damage to Singapore-US ties; and four strokes to preserve the integrity of the system here".

Nevertheless, the government had moved from a position of absolute certainty to one that was open to negotiation, a position that "will no doubt be tested in the future by other parties with real or imagined grievances".

Some of the columns dealt principally with the US media's coverage of the Fay issue.

Writing in *The Sunday Times* on 8 May, Warren Fernandez focused on two examples. The first was New York *Newsday's* decision to run on the front page an account by one Irving Soto, who alleged that he had witnessed public floggings in Singapore several years ago.

This was a very strange story, indeed, for Singapore has no public caning. The paper appeared to have carried it without contacting anyone who could challenge the truth of this tale.

True, it ran a report a few days later calling the story "highly suspect".

"But, I wonder, how many of the other newspapers in America, Australia and elsewhere that picked up the story also published the clarification? And how many readers noticed it?" Fernandez asked.

The second example was Cable News Network's "Larry King Live" programme, which allowed American teenager Dan Noonan and his mother Jeanne to lambast Singapore, alleging that Fay and several other American students had been beaten by the police.

King allowed them to say what they liked, each assertion being taken as fact. Singapore's proconsul, American lawyer Steven Young, tried to press the young man to name the boys who said that they had been abused in Singapore. Fay's American lawyer, Mr

Theodore Simon, responded that it was common knowledge that the police in Singapore beat people.

"Again, assertion to fact, no questions asked." Indeed, it transpired on the show that Mr Noonan had never discussed the case with Fay.

However, an American called from Singapore to put things in perspective. "I have come across American kids, about the same age, who have been going around saying that the Marines are going to land here, and take them all away," she said.

Fernandez commented that this kind of fare called into question the credibility of "the manifold accounts of tyranny and abuse, filed by self-appointed Western vigilantes the world over".

It was the US media — which largely appeared to be concerned neither with Fay himself nor with the legal details of his case — which prompted me to ask in a column what the issue was actually all about.

"Going by the emerging direction of some comments in the US press, Fay, it turns out, is actually a political victim, and the case is about human rights in Singapore."

The pattern apparent in the commentaries was that an American had been sentenced to caning. That caning was part of a larger body of laws. Those laws, in turn, were part of an overall social system. The politics of that system was "dictatorial" or at least "authoritarian". Hence the caning was a political issue.

At a certain level, there was logic in that argument. Laws are made by men. Men live in societies. Politics is the name given to the organization of societies. Thus, all laws are political.

However, if that argument was not applied with discrimination, the results could be ludicrous.

For if every law was political and thus if every sentence was political, a sentence for rape must be a political one. Imprisonment for rape would therefore turn the rapist into a political prisoner.

Looking at the American media's coverage of the issue, I argued, it was difficult to escape the conclusion that human rights had become a convenient weapon for sections of American opinion to set upon systems they did not like, for whatever reason.

One danger in their doing so was that even those who welcomed the heightened international awareness of human rights would argue that turning a conviction for vandalism into a human rights issue trivialized it. At this rate, human rights fatigue would set in. And then who would care for the genuine cases of human rights abuse?

As for Fay, it was one thing to plead for leniency on compassionate grounds. "It is another to try and extract concessions by reviling a system, questioning its political legitimacy and lumping it together dubiously with other systems."

While doing so might afford writers vicarious pleasure, it detracted attention from the actual issue, which should be Fay himself.

American media coverage was the subject of a column by Leslie Fong in *The Straits Times* on 4 June

1994 in which he went on to discuss an important point that had not drawn comment.

Fong wondered whether ordinary Americans would remember that some of their journalists were "doing a hatchet job on Singapore". He was not certain. A great number of Americans who supported Singapore did so because they were tired of rising crime in their cities. If the situation changed, their ideas of caning might change, too.

Would they then remember Singapore as a country that had bloodied American buttocks, not one that had applied the law equally?

If they did, the media campaign against Singapore would have caused the greatest damage.

"At the end of the day, no thanks to all that slanted reporting and commentary, the average American, who is not exactly well-informed about the world and probably still thinks this country is part of China, will associate Singapore with repression and brutality," Fong said.

As for the American intellectual elite, they were unlikely to defend Singapore's action, which they see as a challenge to their liberal ideas of society and governance.

"To the extent that Singapore needs the goodwill of Americans in high places, who have to pay heed to what their press and their voters think and say", Fong argued, it was important for Singaporeans to engage their American friends or business contacts at a personal level about the issues thrown up in the Fay controversy.

Cherian George had a different idea of how this could be done. In a break from the serious, and sometimes angry, tone of previous commentaries, he had a hilarious suggestion in a TV watch column on 29 May.

Describing a recently-televised "Wrestlemania X" programme, he drew on the moral of the stage-managed wrestling saga.

"Wrestlemania is guileless, undisguised propaganda.

"It is a platform for Americans to play out their fantasies, a vent for pent-up emotions.

"It is sometimes racist, and often crudely nationalistic.

"It is a way for Americans to rewrite history, reshape current affairs, and get their own back against forces that their government seems helpless to do anything about."

If a televised wrestling match was a safety-valve that enabled Americans to vent their frustrations instead of going to war, it could provide Singapore a way of making irate Americans get rid of their anger.

The Singaporean "sacrificial lamb" would wear blue policeman's trousers and enter the arena with a long cane, which he would hand to his manager, Mr Ban Chew Gum.

Yes, the Singaporean wrestler would be called Mr Cane. He could be the next performance artist booked on obscenity charges — or Dick Lee.

During the match, American youth with spray cans and their parents would scream abuse till they were hoarse.

The Media War

The American wrestler would pound Mr Cane to a pulp.

Singaporeans in the crowd would then "acknowledge graciously that the Americans are in all ways bigger and better. They could take the pacified Americans out for a beer".

"Then everyone could go home friends.

And, one hopes, things will be quiet again."

The idea that a sufficiently cathartic spectacle might provide a relatively painless denouement for the episode is apt in many ways. However, some have criticized the Singapore media for hardening the public's attitudes to the issue. Critics asked privately why the papers had decided to "play up" the case in the first place. Why, for example, did *The Straits Times* give front-page coverage to the case when the police made arrests? After all, it was not the paper's normal practice to highlight cases of vandalism and mischief in this way; even murder stories did not always get such prominent coverage.

Then, why was a report on vandalism highlighted by the use of a picture showing graffiti-riddled walls, when Fay had had nothing to do with that act of vandalism? Was this not a transparent effort to whip up public sentiment against him and the other alleged offenders? Why, if so? Was it because they were foreigners? Were the papers "picking on" these teenagers because they were foreigners, and trying to turn public opinion against them? Were they warning Singapore's youth not to go the way of these teenagers, some of whom came from the "decadent" West?

Indeed, one Singaporean wondered in a private conversation whether it was *The Straits Times* that should be held responsible for whipping up public interest to a degree that shrank the government's room for manoeuvre in dealing with US criticism of the punishment.

A Western journalist, not an American, working in Singapore went further. He felt that it was "a piece of hypocrisy" for the media to claim that the Western press had blown the issue out of proportion when Singapore's press itself had turned a comparatively minor incident into front page news. Why? He surmised that an "arrogant self-satisfaction" had driven Singapore to try and teach the world how superior its laws were, and how destructive was the American "laissez-faire attitude to crime". That superior attitude was a cultural, not a racial, one, but it was driven nevertheless by a "messianic" zeal.

Strong words. Were they justified?

Leslie Fong, Editor of *The Straits Times*, disagrees. In an interview, he defended the paper's coverage of the case by saying that the punishment of expatriate children was expected to arouse "exactly the kind of sentiments that we saw" later.

"We knew instinctively that the story would not end with the court judgment but that there would be a political fallout and there indeed was a political fallout, though far more severe than what we had imagined.

"It was what any professional editor would have done. We went strictly on the merits of the story."

The Media War

As for the charge that the papers' coverage pushed the government into a corner, Fong replied bluntly: "I don't think that the Singapore government operates according to what is published in *The Straits Times*."

Yes, the government is responsive to public opinion, and the paper did to an extent generate public opinion by publishing the story. However, he said, the government's handling of the issue would not have changed even if the story had not been published. In any case, in a country of Singapore's size, it was impossible that the teenagers' actions would have gone unnoticed if the paper had not reported on them the way it had done.

Indeed, the public interest demanded that the media report on the issue. "This is our country. As a national newspaper, we consider it part of our duty to speak up on things that affect public life. We will not countenance foreign interference in our domestic affairs, certainly not foreign attempts to subvert justice in Singapore.

"All that we care about is that the law be applied equally. We do not want a Singapore that treats its citizens in one way and foreigners, be they Americans or Zulus, in another. If we give up that principle, we may as well close shop, for this place would not be worth having."

That said, Fong argued, the paper's editorials were "correct, dignified and proper", not strident, sensational or jingoistic — "which is more than I can say for some parts of the American media".

Similarly, the paper's columns were "nowhere near the hysterical pitch" evident in some US papers and did not try to arouse anti-American sentiments among Singaporeans.

"We consider it beneath our dignity to trade insults.

"We were professional. We sifted fact from fantasy. We observed standards of fairness, accuracy and balance."

Chua Huck Cheng, who penned its editorials on the Fay issue, adopted a slightly different approach in defending its coverage and commentary.

"If some expatriate children have a certain propensity not to observe proper rules of conduct, then it is perfectly all right for a newspaper to give that fact publicity.

"It is a means of nipping a problem at source."

As for the media reducing the government's room for manoeuvre, it was "the US media and special interests which warped the issue. If at all, our reporting put the spotlight on this so as to set out in clearer terms how the Singapore government could respond".

He himself would have preferred the paper to have adopted a "slightly patronizing" editorial tone in commenting on the fact that "here was the most important politician in the world getting involved in a trifling matter", but the paper's tone was "not hostile".

"We were trying to find a middle-ground to take the sting out of the incident", though after the American columnists and lobbies intervened, the tone became tougher.

The Media War

"We had to fight fire with fire," Chua said.

In the same way, the columns were "focused", replying to particular points raised by US columnists and trying to set the context. "We were restrained in the face of some pretty gratuitous insults."

Overall, the object lesson of the Fay affair was that "a section of the US media does not want to accept certain truths if these do not fit its preconceived notions".

"We do not have to justify ourselves to them," he argued.

***

The Singapore media was essentially reactive. This contrasted with the American media, whose nationalist agenda made it try and turn Fay into a national symbol. By most accounts, this did not cut much ice. However, it worked in the sense that it made the US Administration intervene on his behalf. Singapore's government had to respond.

To the official sphere we now turn.

CHAPTER III
OFFICIAL RESPONSES

WHAT IS INTERESTING is that, unlike the US media's efforts to turn Fay into a human rights issue, the US government treated his case as basically a consular matter. The distinction is an important one. The American media's coverage suggested that Singapore was making an example of Fay to warn its own youth of the dangers of Western decadence, as exemplified in America's over-lenient penal system and the consequent disregard of criminals for the law. It was also said that Fay was the victim of a rising Asian assertiveness towards the West and the Asian claim, made at the UN human rights conference in Vienna, that the Western concept of human rights was not a universal one. Some commentators related Singapore's actions to China's rise in world affairs and the avowed effects of this on the perceptions of Singapore's majority community. Fay was portrayed as a human rights victim in Chinese-majority Singapore at a time when Americans were reading daily about the human rights situation in China.

The US government, by contrast, treated the Fay issue as a legal and not a political one, though, in doing so, it nevertheless left itself open to charges that it was trying to interfere in Singapore's judicial system. It is worthwhile to see how the issue unfolded, what arguments Washington used to argue its case and how the Singapore government responded.

As for the Singapore government, it viewed the issue as a judicial one. Once the Fay case was before the courts, there was nothing the government could do to respond to US criticism of the severity of the sentence for vandalism.

There was another factor. The US Administration's public utterances were undoubtedly driven by a need to respond to the uproar created by the US press, which subjected the Singapore government, and the values it stood for, to hysterical attacks. It was the need to reply to those attacks that led, as we shall see, Cabinet ministers from mid-April onwards to defend the Singapore system publicly. In the process, they compared it with the US system, pointing out the latter's manifold problems — something they had not done till then. The point here is that there is nothing to show that the Singapore authorities wanted to use the case to illustrate what had gone wrong with America's penal and broader social system. It was only when the US media tried to use the case to illustrate what they found unacceptable about Singapore's system that its ministers spoke up.

The first public response by the US Embassy in Singapore to the Fay case came on 3 March 1994, when he was sentenced in the District Court. Speaking to reporters outside the court, US Chargé d'Affaires Ralph Boyce acknowledged that "American citizens overseas, as guests in the host country, are subject to the laws of that country". What the embassy wanted to do was to "ensure that his legal rights under Singapore law were accorded to him".

That was a significant phrase: Fay's rights under Singapore law were what the embassy was concerned with. This was "standard practice" for any American residing abroad. Mr Boyce was not questioning the right of Singapore's courts to pass judgment on Fay. He also acknowledged that Fay had had an attorney of his own choosing and that the proceedings had been held in public court.

However, he commented that, in the outcome of the case, "we see a large discrepancy between the offence and the punishment. The cars were not permanently damaged; the paint was removed with thinner. Caning leaves permanent scars".

Moreover, Fay was a teenager and this was his first offence. "The US Embassy has informed the Singapore Government of our concern regarding this case on a number of occasions. We have made our concerns clear regarding this type of punishment for a youthful first-time offender."

And then came the sting. "We are not going to forecast any possible future diplomatic actions," Mr Boyce said.

It was a carefully phrased statement. It sought to balance US recognition of Singapore's right to uphold its laws with its concerns over the particular punishment. But the reference to possible diplomatic actions in the future revealed US disquiet and set the tone for what would follow. What was equally, if not more, significant was that the American diplomat had gone public with his comments.

The Ministry of Home Affairs responded the same day, and both the content and the tone of that response made clear its displeasure over Mr Boyce's statement.

"Unlike some other societies which may tolerate acts of vandalism," it said, "Singapore has its own standards of social order as reflected in our laws.

"It is because of our tough laws against antisocial crimes that we are able to keep Singapore orderly and relatively crime-free.

"We do not have a situation where acts of vandalism are commonplace, as in cities like New York where even police cars are not spared."

The statement drew attention to the fact that Singaporeans and foreigners were subject to the same laws in Singapore. In the past five years, out of 14 people aged 18 to 21 who had been convicted of vandalism and ordered to be caned, 12 had been Singaporeans.

"The law provides for a range of punishments to meet the varying degrees of seriousness of an offence and the circumstances under which it was committed. It is the court that decides on the appropriate punishment to fit the crime."

After discussing the Fay case, it said that Singapore expected its citizens to follow the laws of the countries they visit or reside in. "Similarly, we also expect foreigners in Singapore to abide by our laws."

The Ministry of Foreign Affairs, it added, had

informed the embassy that "the law in Singapore must take its course".

Matters escalated when, at a press conference in Washington on 7 March 1994, President Clinton intervened publicly in the affair.

"We recognize that they have a certain right to enforce their own criminal laws," he said, "but we believe that, based on the facts and the treatment of other cases, similar cases, that this punishment is extreme, and we hope very much that somehow it will be reconsidered." He added that the US had filed "a strong protest" with Singapore.

Again, the US recognized Singapore's right to uphold its laws, but the use of the words "a certain" suggested that the recognition was a qualified one. Singapore, the President was implying, had the right to enforce its laws as long as these did not fall foul of certain standards, which he did not mention. Instead, he spoke of his concerns over the severity of the sentence.

Similarly, he hoped that it would "somehow" be reconsidered, but without suggesting how. Since Fay had been sentenced in court — and was planning to appeal — how could the Singapore government intervene in the due process of law without undermining that process? Indeed, what was the point in having the government's right to uphold the legal system recognized if, by interfering in that system, it were to undermine it?

The US Embassy conveyed its concerns to the Ministry of Foreign Affairs the same day. The following day, 8 March 1994, a Ministry's spokesman said what its response to the embassy had been. He reiterated that "the law in Singapore must take its course" and that the ministry "cannot be expected to intervene in the due process of the law". Without naming President Clinton, he called incorrect the statement that based on the facts and the treatment of other cases, similar cases, the punishment had been extreme.

To make its point that the sentence on him was "neither extreme nor unprecedented", it described three previous cases of vandalism, and appended a comparative table of 14 cases between 1989 and 1993.

Fay's appeal was heard and dismissed by the Chief Justice on 31 March. Mr Boyce took questions from reporters outside the Supreme Court Building. He expressed regret that the Appeal Court's decision "leaves in place the caning element" of the sentence. The embassy continued to believe that caning was an "excessive penalty for a youthful nonviolent offender who pleaded guilty to reparable crimes against private property" and continued to hope that the government would reconsider the sentence to cane Fay, whose lawyer was making an appeal for presidential clemency.

Asked whether the US was interfering in Singapore's internal affairs, he replied that it was the business of the US to look after its citizens. "At the same time, of course, we reiterated time and again that we understand that our citizens abroad are subject to the laws of the countries in which they reside." However, caning was an excessive penalty "in this case".

Those comments drew a brisk rejoinder from the

Ministry of Home Affairs. It was surprised, a statement said, that Mr Boyce had expressed his regrets on the court's decision. "This is the second time he has criticized the judgment of a Singapore court in public. This is regrettable.

"As a diplomat accredited to Singapore, and representing a country that respects the rule of law, he should respect Singapore's judicial system. There are official channels for him to make representations."

The statement repeated details of the Fay case.

April was a hectic month in the evolution of the affair.

Early that month, 24 US Senators signed a letter, circulated on Capitol Hill by Senators Howard Metzenbaum and John Glenn, both Democrats of Ohio, appealing to President Ong Teng Cheong for clemency for Fay.

They said that he had a history of emotional problems; severe corporal punishment could create psychological damage that would take years to repair.

In Singapore, visiting Republican Senator William Cohen disclosed that he had discussed the case with Senior Minister Lee Kuan Yew and Deputy Prime Minister Brigadier-General (NS) Lee Hsien Loong.

He said he had expressed concern to them that Fay was being singled out for special treatment. However, both had "clearly indicated that this is not the case" and that it was a judicial matter.

"I gathered from the leadership that they're not going to yield," he revealed. "They resent the West telling them what they should do and they're obviously ready to take the consequences."

What was the bottomline?

"It has become a test of wills. Will Singapore yield to the pressure from the US? The answer is no."

It was reported around this time that Singapore had received a letter from President Clinton to President Ong pleading for clemency for Fay.

It appeared at the time that this was about all there was to the issue as far as the US government was concerned. On 10 April, Secretary of State Warren Christopher said that trade would not be affected if Singapore went ahead with the sentence. On 13 April, asked by a reporter whether the US government felt that it had done everything possible to prevent the caning, State Department spokesman Michael McCurry said: "Yes."

However, the very next day, President Clinton made his second intervention in the affair when he said at a news conference that it would be a mistake for Singapore to cane Fay.

Many Americans who had expressed sympathy for the caning did not understand the brutality of it, he thought. "He is going to bleed considerably and may have permanent scars, and I think it is a mistake."

He added that he remained undecided about whether to call on US corporations doing business in Singapore to pressure the government.

Referring to former President George Bush, who was travelling to Singapore to address a business leaders' conference, Mr Clinton said that if Mr Bush decided to "say something supportive of the absence of caning, I would certainly be grateful".

(In Singapore, Mr Bush told a group of students that he opposed caning because it was brutal, but he gave no hint that he might intercede on Fay's behalf.)

Then, on 19 April, President Clinton made his third intervention in the affair during an MTV interview with young Americans.

"As you know, I have spoken out against his punishment for two reasons. One is it's not entirely clear that his confession wasn't coerced from him.

"The second is that if he just were to serve four months in prison for what he did, that would be quite severe. But the caning may leave permanent scars, and some people who are caned in the way they are caned there go into shock. I mean, it's much more serious than it sounds."

The first point provided an important perspective on the issue. Allegations of police brutality towards Fay had appeared sporadically in the US media; a report had said that he had told his friends and family that the police had abused him physically and had coerced him into signing a false confession.

It was interesting, therefore, that President Clinton should voice that allegation publicly, albeit in an indirect way, as late as on 19 April, even as the outcome of his appeal to President Ong for clemency was pending.

With that comment, the circumstances in which Fay had confessed took on a higher profile.

Official Responses

In a letter to the *International Herald Tribune* later that month, Mr Nathan noted, without mentioning the President, that the US Embassy had complained in October 1993 that Fay had been abused during police questioning. The Ministry of Home Affairs had made an investigation and had found no evidence of police abuse, he said. The US Embassy had received a full account of the investigation, but it had not pursued the matter further, he wrote.

In Singapore, Cabinet ministers had become increasingly vocal on the caning sentence since mid-April.

Mr Lee Kuan Yew said on SBC's current affairs programme, "Face to Face", that the US reaction to the caning issue illustrated that America did not dare restrain or punish individuals who did wrong.

It was the world's richest country, but it was "hardly safe and peaceful".

The US government, the Senate and the media had used the Fay incident to ridicule Singapore, saying that the punishment was too severe, but Singapore's stand was that the government must protect society. If it did not, there would be chaos.

"If you like it this way, that is your problem," he said. "But that is not the path we choose."

That comment drew attention to an interesting aspect of the issue. Throughout the affair, the response of Singapore's leadership made it clear that, unlike Americans who could not accept the punishment because it did not fit in with their own legal system,

Singapore was not suggesting that the US should have caning because Singapore did.

(As Mr Nathan had written to the *International Herald Tribune* in March 1994, "we claim no universal validity for our approach to law and order".)

All it was saying was that the presence of caning as a punishment served the Republic well.

Thus, at a press conference in Canberra on 20 April, Mr Lee said that while foreigners might consider Singapore's punishments barbaric, what mattered was that the penal system had produced conditions in which Singaporeans had been able to prosper.

Indeed, he said, while American columnists tried to tell Singapore's leaders how to run the country, if effective punishments were abolished and there was disorder, US firms would withdraw their investments. Singaporeans, too, might choose to send their money and their families to safer places abroad.

The point: Singapore's laws must fit Singapore's realities.

On 23 April, Home Affairs Minister Wong Kan Seng defended caning as a form of punishment. Laws would not be effective if the penalties for flouting them were not sufficiently strict, he said.

He did not refer directly to allegations that Fay had been coerced into confessing his crimes, but he emphasized that enforcement officers would be punished if any complaint against them was substantiated.

"The Government will not allow an occasional black sheep who abuses his powers to undermine the integrity and reputation of our law enforcement agencies and system."

In an interview published in *The Baltimore Sun* on 25 April, Health, and Information and the Arts Minister Brigadier-General (NS) George Yeo said that the government would lose its moral authority if it granted President Clinton's request for clemency for Fay.

"If we are seen buckling in to media pressure or to political pressure from America, then it is no longer possible for us to govern Singapore. We become a joke. It is not possible. We lose all moral authority."

B-G Yeo denied that Singapore was making an example out of Fay. Caning, he argued, was vital to maintaining law and order in the Republic.

"There must be an effectiveness to the deterrent. You cannot cane someone and expect it to be painless. What is the deterrent value? You might as well give him a book to read."

On 4 May, Law and Foreign Affairs Minister Professor S. Jayakumar told an international gathering of lawyers in Singapore that what was at stake in the controversy was not caning as a form of punishment, but whether one country should respect the right of another to enact and enforce its own laws.

"If today we are told that we are not entitled to cane, then tomorrow we will be told that we cannot enforce the death penalty, and on some other day, that we cannot enforce some other law," he said.

Responding to the "vitriolic" attacks on Singapore by some newspapers, columnists and politicians in the

US, he said they had failed to realize that no Singapore government could govern effectively if its citizens saw their leaders as having succumbed to US press pressure.

Indeed, even the US Embassy had acknowledged, in its March Productivity Report, that Singapore had "a transparent legal and business environment" and that "its low crime rate is the envy of richer countries".

***

Later that day, a government press statement said that the Cabinet had advised President Ong to reduce Fay's caning sentence from six to four strokes.

Fay had petitioned the President to commute his caning; President Clinton, too, had written to President Ong, it said. The Cabinet, in its review of the merits of the case, the statement added, had found no special circumstances which could justify commuting the caning sentence. But it valued Singapore's good relations with the US and Washington's constructive economic and security role in the region.

"To reject his appeal totally would show an unhelpful disregard for the President and the domestic pressures on him on this issue."

Singapore hoped that the reduction would "go some way to meeting President Clinton's concern".

This was being done "without compromising the principle that persons convicted of vandalism must be caned".

The reduction in the sentence was an exceptional decision which would not be a precedent for future

Official Responses

cases, the statement added.

The White House reacted with disappointment to Singapore's decision. "We believe the punishment is out of step with the crime. We believe the government knows our position on that," its spokesman, Dee Dee Myers, said.

Fay was caned on 5 May 1994.

Washington's response was to summon Mr Nathan. Assistant Secretary of State Winston Lord told him that the President was very disappointed, to which the Ambassador replied: "I'm disappointed that the US government should feel disappointed."

Mr Lord said that the State Department would shortly be reissuing its consular information sheet warning Americans considering travelling to Singapore that they would be subject to harsh punishment under its laws if convicted of crimes.

He also emphasized that the incident would have to be taken into account in the overall relationship between the US and Singapore.

However, Vice-President Al Gore said that while Washington was disappointed with Singapore's decision, it would "move on".

"It's disappointing. It happened. We are looking at the situation, but we move on from here," he said, adding that strong relations with Singapore continued to be important to both countries.

In Singapore, Prime Minister Goh Chok Tong said on 7 May that as far as the Singapore government was concerned, "the episode is closed".

It appeared for a moment that retaliation was on its way when Trade Representative Mickey Kantor said on 9 May that the US would resist Singapore's offer to host the first meeting of the World Trade Organization. Singapore replied that the choice of venue was up to the members of the organization, not to Mr Kantor.

However, the fact that Singapore's decision had mollified the Administration, even though it might not have satisfied it, was made clear during the Senate confirmation hearing of Timothy Chorba, ambassador-designate to Singapore, less than two weeks after the caning. Early into the hearing, chaired by Senator Charles Robb, Democrat of Virginia, Mr Chorba said:

"On occasion we have differences with nations with which we otherwise enjoy good relations, and Singapore is no exception. A recent example is the case of Michael Fay, who was caned in Singapore. Both President Clinton and Secretary of State Christopher have objected to the severity of the sentence. If the Senate confirms my nomination in the aftermath of this incident, I would draw upon my years of practical international experience to represent our nation in charting the course of its relations with the Republic of Singapore, a country of substantial strategic, commercial and political significance to the United States."

In a single paragraph — as it appears in the unofficial transcript distributed by the United States Information Service — Mr Chorba bridged two imperatives. One was the Fay affair, the importance of which to the US government he acknowledged. The other was the depth of America's relations with Singapore, a country of substantial importance to it. The first imperative would not overshadow the second.

He went on to give details. Singapore was America's tenth largest trading partner and its eleventh largest export market, absorbing about US$13 billion of American products every year. About 900 US companies were based in the Republic, and 10,000 Americans lived there.

Singapore was also of "considerable military significance" to the US. It commanded a strategic position on the sea lanes between the Far East and the Indian Ocean. The US Navy had a logistics unit there, and the US Air Force carried out rotating deployments of fighter aircraft in Singapore.

The Republic played a major role in regional security and economic arrangements. It was the home of the Secretariat of the Asia-Pacific Economic Cooperation grouping and was a "pivotal" member of Asean.

The hearing turned to Fay's caning. Senator Robb asked Mr Chorba what the Administration's policy was regarding the first meeting of the World Trade Organization, which Mr Kantor had said should not be held in Singapore. The Ambassador-elect replied that the position was that the site of the meeting should be left to the members of the organization — a reply which mirrored Singapore's response to Mr Kantor's comment.

Pressed to clarify whether the US position on the venue was related to the caning, he replied: "I believe, Senator, that the US position on this issue is not related to the caning incident."

Asked whether the State Department was conducting a formal review of relations with Singapore following the caning, Mr Chorba repeated Mr Lord's statement that the incident would have to be taken into account in the overall relationship. He said that he was not aware of any "explicit measures" that may have been agreed upon, saying only that the incident "has certainly had an impact on public perception of Singapore, and that's something that'll have to be taken into consideration up the road".

However, what was the most newsworthy point of the session was what Mr Chorba said in response to the Senator's question on whether it would be appropriate for the Administration to re-evaluate the sale of F-18 Hornet jetfighters to Singapore.

"The sale of the F-18 is one which would be in America's national interest," Mr Chorba replied, adding that the Administration would favour proceeding with the sale of the F-18s or F-16s, whichever Singapore selected.

A Department of Defence memorandum released later underlined the point. "This sale would contribute to the foreign policy and national security of the United States by helping to improve the security of a friendly country which has been and continues to be an important force for economic progress in Southeast Asia."

***

It was obvious that Singapore's decision to reduce Fay's sentence was successful in preventing a single incident from turning into a focal point in its relationship with the US and clouding the many factors which underpin it.

Given the pressures on it over the issue, the US Administration needed to do something. Given its record for consistency and its citizens' feelings, so did the Singapore government. The reduction was criticized by those Singaporeans who had supported the sentence because they felt that the government had stepped back in the face of US pressure. It was criticized by American newspapers which were against the caning sentence. But it achieved damage-limitation, often a critical challenge in diplomacy.

The government had a tricky problem on its hands. On the one hand, it had to uphold the reality of its judicial system as a way of upholding its sovereignty, for what is sovereignty without the ability to uphold laws? On the other hand, the world of international relations is a world of realpolitik. In it, all states are equal because they are sovereign. But that equality is a legal one. In actuality, the system is very unequal: witness the United Nations' Security Council, in which the five nuclear haves are permanent members holding the veto over the affairs of the world. Small states like Singapore, charting a course in a world where even larger states cannot afford to ignore how powerful states behave, could not but consider its relations with the US in deciding on the outcome of Fay's appeal for clemency to the President. For the government not to have done so would have meant ignoring its duty.

CHAPTER IV
BILATERAL BONDS

THE VAST BACKDROP against which Singapore took a decision on Fay was its relations with the US. These are an intrinsic part of its foreign policy as a small state in a world dominated by major powers.

Former Foreign Minister S. Rajaratnam was a leading exponent of Singapore's views. Combining a capacity for deep analysis with a trademark wit and humour, he explained in speech after speech what Singapore needed to do to make its way in the world.

In an address to the Asia Society in New York in 1973, he said that Singapore accepted power politics as a fact of international politics. It had been that way for the past thousand years and it would remain that way for the next thousand years. Small nations would have to accept the fact of "great power influence and even manipulation".

He employed a metaphor to make his point. "Like the sun the great powers will, by their very existence, radiate gravitational power. But if there are many suns then the smaller planets can, by judicious balancing of pulls and counter-pulls, enjoy a greater freedom of movement and a wider choice of options than if they had only one sun around which to revolve.

"The alternative to one-power dominance of the

region is free and peaceful competition by a multiplicity of powers. It's for the good of the great powers. It's good for nimble-footed small nations who understand the game. It's good for peace."

That, in a nutshell, was Singapore's approach: it was to encourage the presence of all the great powers — the US, the Soviet Union, Japan and China — in Southeast Asia. Hence its opposition to excluding the Soviet Union or China from the region because they were communist. The point was that, whatever their domestic political systems, they should be allowed to participate in the affairs of the region as long as they played a stabilizing role.

But within this matrix, the US came to occupy a special place in Singapore's foreign relations. The relationship was marked by a remarkable confluence of political, economic and strategic interests.

***

Ironically, ties had got off to a bad start. In some views, independent Singapore's early anti-Americanism was necessitated by its desire to find acceptance in the Afro-Asian bloc and support for its bid to join the United Nations. Those views are unduly cynical.

Certain US actions appeared to betray an ignorance of, and arrogance towards, Asian mores that infuriated Singapore's young leaders.

Also, the excesses in Vietnam — stemming from a primary failure to distinguish nationalists from communists — appeared to confirm the view that America was a fickle hegemon at best, bereft of the deep historical insights which the European powers, for all their wickedness, had brought to their imperial enterprise. In August 1965, Mr Lee was quoted as having said: "It is fundamental. If the British bases go, there will be no American bases in Singapore."

Nevertheless, relations changed dramatically just two years into Singapore's independence. The reasons were political, economic and strategic.

Politically, much had to do with the Vietnam war, on which the Republic's stand changed, though it was not a *volte-face*. Singapore now argued that the US had been ill-advised to have become involved in Vietnam, but that, having done so, it should not make a precipitate withdrawal since that would leave all those who depended on it in the lurch. Indeed, there was the feeling that, for all its misguided enthusiasm, the American intervention in Vietnam had provided non-communist Southeast Asian nations with crucial breathing space to consolidate their independence and achieve stability.

Thus, on a visit to the US in 1967, Mr Lee remarked that "if Southeast Asia goes, then in the course of the next decade or two, the whole of South Asia right up to Iran could go communist". It was clarified on his return that this was not meant to be an endorsement of US policy in Vietnam, but a statement of Singapore's expectations of the American role in Southeast Asia.

It was a significant trip; according to a commentator, Mr Lee had succeeded in convincing President

Lyndon Johnson that Chinese Singaporeans were Singaporeans first and last, thereby assuaging American suspicions that the city-state might become a communist base because of its ethnic composition.

In subsequent years, Singapore's leadership would not only keep impressing on the Americans the need to stay engaged in Southeast Asia, but criticize half-hearted supporters of the US in the region. Following the fall of Saigon, Singapore said that "our problem is not persuading the Soviet Union to maintain a presence but persuading the United States and the Western powers".

In his 1973 Asia Society speech, which was on Southeast Asia after Vietnam, Mr Rajaratnam said that "fairly reliable guesses" could be made about the Soviet Union and China. What were America's intentions?

In asking this question, he noted the irony of the fact that though totalitarian societies were secretive about their day-to-day actions, they were open about their long-term goals and their strategies for getting there. By contrast, America's intentions were uncertain in spite of its being a democracy and having a free press — and perhaps precisely because of these, for in a democracy comments about foreign policy are often made more with an eye on domestic politics than because of their intrinsic value.

The Foreign Minister distinguished between two kinds of US intervention in Southeast Asia. The first had been unsuccessful; the second could be successful. The first was its intervention in an anti-colonial war in Vietnam.

"Essentially the Americans took on an anti-colonial war, which the French had already abandoned as lost. They stepped in in the mistaken belief that they were aborting Russian and later Chinese designs to take over the country," he argued.

"Today we know better. Anti-colonial wars are unbeatable. The French, the British and the Dutch learnt it at great cost... Vietnam is the last of the classical anti-colonial wars in Southeast Asia," Mr Rajaratnam said.

But there was a second kind of intervention which was possible, and Americans were unbeatable in the skills and resources which it called for. "The second intervention requires the massive export and deployment of modern technological skills, financial resources, industrial expertise and commercial and organizational know-how — and these the Americans possess in abundance. If this is the contest — and this should have been the contest right from the start — then America has an assured future in Southeast Asia."

The reference to the US as an economic leader for the region tied in with Singapore's own policies for rapid industrialization. These policies were crucial for the survival and success of a small state which was without natural resources and which had been forced into a precipitate independence. Economic realities determined the political choices Singapore made, and naturally so. In those choices, the US loomed large.

The Republic's leaders spoke at length about its economic options. A 1972 speech by Mr Rajaratnam on Singapore as a Global City brought the strands together. The reason why independent Singapore had not gone down the drain was that it was transforming itself into a Global City, though it continued to be a regional entrepôt serving the economies of its neighbours. Global cities "are linked intimately with one another. Because they are more alike they reach out to one another through the tentacles of technology. Linked together they form a chain of cities which today shape and direct, in varying degrees of importance, a worldwide system of economics."

Commenting on Singapore's lack of an economic hinterland, he acknowledged that if the city-state had been no more than a self-contained regional city, it would have got into trouble after independence. "But once you see Singapore as a Global City the problem of hinterland becomes unimportant because for a Global City, the world is its hinterland."

Singapore was becoming a component of a global system, increasingly linked to other global cities by sea, by air and through the international financial network. But "the strongest evidence" of Singapore's role, Mr Rajaratnam said, was the way it was linking up with international and multinational corporations.

These corporations not only brought much-needed investment to the host countries, but they introduced them to high technology and advanced managerial and marketing skills. By linking up with them, Singapore would not only become a component of the world economy, but it could take "a short-cut" to catch up with the most advanced countries.

This is where the US was important: its multinational corporations were world leaders. As Mr Rajaratnam noted wryly, US multinationals abroad had been described as the third largest economy in the world after the United States and the Soviet Union!

That free-trade policy became a cornerstone of Singapore's success.

Today, some things have changed, but others have not. There is a distinct move towards regionalization in trade in Europe, the American continent and Asia, where Japan's prowess, the rise of China and economic liberalization in Vietnam and India are leading to changing patterns of investment and trade flows. These point to deepening intra-regional links and less dependence on the West as a source of capital and a destination for exports.

However, the US remains a key player. In the case of Singapore, it absorbs 20 per cent of its exports, and the 900 US companies in the Republic employ a substantial number of workers.

This is part of America's general economic presence in the region and its leadership in world economic affairs.

Strategically, after its withdrawal from continental Southeast Asia after the fall of Saigon in 1975, US military ties with East Asia centred on its bilateral defence treaties with Tokyo, Seoul and Manila. These treaties were not only important to the three countries. They provided the US a permanent foothold in Asia and, together with the mobile presence of the Seventh Fleet, created an overall climate of stability and confidence which benefited the non-communist countries of Southeast Asia, including Singapore.

However, there were problems with a continuing US military presence even before the collapse of the Soviet Union. A protectionist mood was enveloping America in response not only to its reduced military vulnerability as the Soviet empire wound down, but also to its growing economic problems, seen in its burgeoning federal and trade deficits.

Many Americans not only argued that their country could no longer afford its extensive military engagements abroad, they said that it did not make sense for Washington to bear the financial responsibility for protecting its Asian allies — Japan, South Korea and the Philippines — when the Japanese and the Koreans were responsible for a sizeable portion of the US trade deficit. As Americans sarcastically asked: What was the US defending in Japan and Korea? Its trade deficit with them?

Indeed, they asked, would the Asian dynamos have turned into such lean and mean exporting machines if they had needed to devote a large part of their resources to defence? Would they have been able then to channel money and human skills into developing their export industries? Was it not the US military umbrella that enabled them to take a free ride on defence? What the isolationists demanded to know was why US military expenditure — a major part of its budget deficit — should finance its trade deficit.

Of course, these arguments were simplistic. In strategic terms, the US bases in Japan, South Korea and the Philippines not only defended those countries but also defended America. Confronted by the Sino-Soviet bloc after World War II, the US had adopted a forward defence strategy whose premise was that if permanent US forces, along with their local allies, could fight a Soviet or Soviet-sponsored attack in Asia itself, American forces would not have to stop Soviet forces in or near continental America itself. In the process, of course, the US would need to defend its allies. It was a two-way street.

In financial terms, America's military spending did help protect its economic competitors, but it also contributed to its own economic growth and created jobs for Americans. Military cutbacks, even to the limited extent that occurred after the downfall of the Soviet Union, led to demobilization, the closure of bases and the inevitable impact on the US defence industry and supporting industries.

In fact, it has been argued that defence expenditure, and even a defence buildup, does not inevitably cause budget deficits, which result from an unwillingness to raise taxes or cut back on other areas of spending sufficiently to finance larger military outlays. The point is to define the optimum level of defence spending. The US, it has been said, can spend between 5 per cent and 10 per cent of its gross national product on defence without throwing its budget into disarray or declining as an economic power.*

---

* Aaron L. Friedburg, "*The Political Economy of U.S. National Security Policy*", in Daniel J. Kaufman, *et al* (eds.), *U.S. National Security Strategy for the 1990s,* The Johns Hopkins University Press, Baltimore and London, 1991, pp. 59-80.

The isolationist argument was, therefore, not correct. But the problem was that it was growing increasingly popular as America's economic problems soared. That bode ill for Asia. If the isolationists won, would a second Saigon occur, less dramatic than the first but in fact even more destructive for those countries which benefited from America's regional presence?

What was worse, the arguments for isolation were often voiced by retired military personnel. The American military presence overseas was based on the need to protect America's strategic interests. If military men, who surely knew what they were talking about, argued that the US did not need to be engaged extensively abroad, what possible justification could there be for doing so?

The arguments for military retrenchment were summed up in testimony which retired Rear-Admiral Gene R. La Rocque, director of the Centre for Defence Information, gave at a hearing of the Defence Burden-sharing Panel of the House of Representatives Committee on Armed Services on 19 April 1988.*

Admiral La Rocque began by mentioning an interesting set of numbers. The US spent US$150 billion a year to defend its European and Asian allies; it had a US$150 billion federal budget deficit; and it suffered from a US$150 billion trade deficit. If the military expenditure were eliminated, the budget deficit could be

---

* *Common Security Interests In The Pacific And How The Cost And Benefits Of Those Interests Are Shared By The U.S. And Its Allies,* U.S. Government Printing Office, Washington, D. C., 1989.

eliminated and resources could be redirected towards commercial research and development with which to attack the trade deficit.

Then came the military argument. The admiral supported America's decision to adopt a forward defence strategy after World War II. But now, he argued, it did not make sense. If the Soviet Union were to attack the US, it would fire its missiles over the forward defence line or send submarines around it. What this meant was that the Philippines, South Korea and Japan did not really defend the US any more. "Basically, it's a one-way street."

Indeed, he argued, nobody was threatening South Korea or the Philippines. As for Japan, its Constitution neither prescribed the size of its conventional forces nor prevented it from going nuclear as long as Japanese forces were labelled "self-defence forces". Japan therefore was quite capable of ensuring its security, in any case without any danger that a threat to its security might affect America's own security. Given that nothing in the US treaties with the three countries obliged it to station a single American soldier on them, "we ought to pull out gradually from all of those countries in the Far East".

Given such arguments, it was obvious that the US Administration had to do something. It could not be seen to be spending vast sums on its presence abroad when its own economy suffered. Yet, as every American statesman knew, large-scale strategic retrenchment from Asia would cause grave instability there and ultimately threaten America's military and economic interests. A new strategy had to be adopted.

That strategy had two aspects. Its first was burden-sharing, in which Japan and South Korea would have to — and did — pay more towards the cost of stationing US forces there. The second was a "places, not bases" strategy. Instead of bases, or a permanent presence that was expensive and manpower-heavy, the US would seek relatively inexpensive, rotational "access" arrangements with regional countries. Indeed, given the nationalist pressure from the Philippines to shut down Clark Air Base and Subic Bay Naval Station, the need for access arrangements became even more acute.

America's friends needed to respond actively to make it easier for it to stay engaged and maintain the regional stability that they benefited from.

On 4 August 1989, Brigadier-General (NS) George Yeo, then Minister of State for Foreign Affairs, told Parliament that Singapore was prepared to allow the US to set up some military facilities to make it easier for the Philippines to continue hosting the American bases at Clark airfield and Subic Bay. A Memorandum of Understanding was signed in November 1990 allowing the US expanded use of military facilities, and during a visit by President George Bush in January 1992, Singapore agreed in principle to accommodate a US naval logistics element from Subic. (Meanwhile, the Philippines had served notice on the US that it would have to vacate Clark and Subic by the end of 1992.)

Singapore's stance confirmed the degree of

confluence between its geopolitical perceptions and those of the US. The reason was basically that the Philippines government was coming under increasing domestic pressure on the American bases; and though all non-communist Southeast Asian countries enjoyed the protection of the US cover, Manila was the only capital to have to bear the political burden of hosting them. The military facilities which Singapore was offering were small, even negligible, in physical terms — all of Singapore could fit into Subic Bay Naval Station — but the move was a symbolic gesture of support for the US presence in Southeast Asia.

Such gestures were necessary because the end of the Cold War was coinciding with a deepening of America's economic problems and strengthening US domestic sentiments in favour of military disengagement abroad and the diversion of saved resources to the domestic economy. By making it easier for the US to remain engaged abroad, beneficiaries of its presence would be furthering their own interests in an era when the domestic mood in the US was in favour of isolationism.

In the Singapore view, the implications of a US withdrawal would be severe. The Soviet Union was effectively out of the race; if the US, too, went, there would be a power vacuum which the existing powers, Japan and China, and the emergent regional powers, India and Vietnam and perhaps Korea, would seek to fill. The result would be instability for Southeast Asia.

Was the power-vacuum theory alarmist? It would

appear not. At the end of the 1980s, Japan, China and India each had the capacity to project power far in excess of all the Asean countries combined. Even with defence taking only one per cent of its gross national product — and that ceiling was not sacrosanct — Japan's defence budget was the third largest in the world. If trade disputes with the US led to the point where they threatened the security relationship, Japan might not be immune to militaristic nationalism, which could lead to an extension of its military reach into Southeast Asia, beginning with naval patrols 1,000 miles to the south.

As for China, the needs of economic modernization did act as a constraint on foreign military activities in the short term, but a modernized China would have the economic infrastructure to underpin a serious quest for global importance, beginning with Southeast Asia, which it considered as falling within its sphere of influence.

Unlike China, whose lack of a blue-water fleet constrained its actions in Southeast Asia for the time being, India already had a powerful navy which, supported by a modernizing, externally-oriented economy, could form a realistic basis of aspirations to leadership in the Indian Ocean and beyond. A revitalized Vietnam and a unified Korea would not easily accept China's, and Japan's, quest for dominance. Asean could not be quarantined from the struggle for supremacy between these powers, which could lead to the formation of adversarial blocs in East Asia.

Singapore's point was not that the emergence of these powers should, or could, be prevented, but that a new regional order should emerge without causing instability. The US presence was a major contribution towards that end because it was the only power capable of holding the balance of power in the region as one order gave way to another.

It was in that context that Singapore's offer allowing the US to use some of its facilities was made.

***

It might appear from this brief survey that the Republic values its relations with its giant partner because the benefits have been one way. That is not true. Singapore-US relations are very much a two-way street.

Politically, Singapore was among a handful of non-communist Asian countries that stood between the ideology of the Soviet Union and China, and the free world that the Americans led. Though these Asian countries cooperated with the US (and Western Europe) in their own interests, their success in achieving and maintaining domestic stability advanced the political goals of the West, including the US.

Economically, American MNCs have been a centrepiece of Singapore's strategy of export-led industrialization. It is also true that the strategy depended on exporting to prosperous Western markets, led by the American market. However, it is equally true that the MNCs came to Singapore because their profit margins here were higher than they would have been at home. Those margins depended not only on Singapore's lower wages, but on its attractive tax and other policies. Harmonious labour relations, dependent on the tripartite system the government fostered, contributed to this attractive atmosphere, as did Singapore's general political stability.

Indeed, the dominance of multinationals in the Republic's economy has drawn questioning glances. One scholar has argued that Singapore's development strategy often failed to ensure technology transfer, foster foreign-indigenous industrial linkages and stimulate competition, "all of which would have boosted Singapore's self-reliance".* It has also been argued that MNCs, which account overwhelmingly for investment in the manufacturing sector, are crowding out small businesses.

Whatever be the validity of such arguments, Singapore has always been an attractive trading partner for the US and continues to be so. The *Singapore Economic Trends Report* published by the US Embassy in January 1994 notes that the Republic maintains almost no import duties or non-tariff barriers to trade. It is a regional commercial hub. It is also a significant consumer market. "As the population is highly exposed to Western media, especially American TV programmes, things American find a welcome following." The value of the US dollar vis-a-vis the Singapore dollar being at an all-time low, US goods and services are more competitive.

---

* Hafiz Mirza, *Multinationals and the Growth of the Singapore Economy,* Croom Helm, London and Sydney, 1986, p.257.

According to the Report, prepared by the embassy's Economic/Political Section and the Foreign Commercial Service, Singapore distributors are generally well-informed about US products and often represent several American product lines at once. Nevertheless, they are always on the lookout for new products to represent. Many have travelled to the US and have extensive experience in dealing with Americans.

"Doing business in Singapore is straightforward, the country is free of corruption, and business is normally conducted in English," it says. "Due to Singapore's open trade policies, excellent transportation and communications infrastructure, and experienced workforce, firms eager to do business in the region find it an excellent gateway to the rapidly growing markets of Southeast Asia."

Strategically, while it is true that the Republic allowed the US increased military access to its facilities in order to preserve the regional stability from which it (like other Southeast Asian nations) benefited, this simultaneously advanced US interests.

This was recognized at a symposium sponsored by the National Defence University in Honolulu on 2 March 1991. Carl Ford, US Deputy Assistant Secretary of Defence for International Security Affairs, noted that Washington's preferred formula was a structure of "cooperative vigilance" for Pacific Asia, a structure "characterized by a growing security partnership between the United States and its friends and allies...founded upon a full partnership, where all parties provide both adequate financial contributions to the common defence needs and a credible degree of self-sufficiency as well".

In his speech, he noted "the superb cooperation with the Republic of Singapore, and its willingness to contribute to the common defence by permitting increased access for US forces to Singaporean military facilities".

There was a price to be paid for that willingness. In spite of its benefits to the region as a whole, the move was initially misunderstood by Singapore's neighbours and aroused a storm of controversy in their media. The misunderstanding centred on the misconception that the Republic was allowing the Americans to set up a base, thus going against the spirit of Southeast Asia being a Zone of Peace, Freedom and Neutrality (ZOPFAN).

Criticism in the Malaysian and Indonesian press was revived when Singapore agreed to accommodate a US naval logistics element from Subic. It went forward in spite of the criticism.

Its stance was vindicated when Indonesia made its maritime facilities in Surabaya available to the US, and Malaysia offered its facilities at Lumut Naval Base in Perak.

What is clear from all this is the extent to which Singapore's and America's interests interlock. While the US presence in Asia benefits Singapore, it benefits other Asian countries, too, and it certainly benefits America. In making it easier for the US to maintain that presence, Singapore acts out of self-interest — an interest that is consonant with its neighbours' — but, again, this helps the US.

It was this convergence of interests that both Singapore and the US had to keep in mind over the Fay issue. Bilateral relations are a two-way street, whether one starts the journey in Singapore or in Washington.

CHAPTER V

TWO MARINES AND A DIPLOMAT

THE DECISION ON FAY was no less than a foreign policy decision for Singapore. For a small state to survive and prosper, it must operate in the margin of possibilities created by the larger members of the international system. Insulation from that system in the name of sovereignty is folly. All states try to manage their international ties judiciously: for a small state, judicious management is a necessity that can become lethal if it trips up while trying to manoeuvre its way round the pitfalls of power politics, which is the politics of international relations.

Equally, however, Singapore has been jealously concerned with upholding its sovereignty — and precisely because if, as a small state, it does not do so, there will soon be little sovereignty to uphold. In assessing the Fay issue in terms of that stance on sovereignty, it may be useful to look at two other incidents, one involving Indonesian marines* and the other an American diplomat. Doing so may dispel the idea that Fay's sentence was reduced because he is an American.

***

---

* In a letter to *The Straits Times*, political scientist, Hussin Mutalib, had recalled this case in commenting on Singapore's decision to reduce Fay's sentence.

Indonesian marines Haroen bin Said and Osman bin Mohammed Ali planted a bomb that exploded in MacDonald House on 10 March 1965. The casualties: three dead and 30 injured. The saboteurs were captured, tried and sentenced to death that year. They appealed all the way to the House of Lords, which dismissed their appeal. They were hanged on 17 October 1968.

The bombing had been part of President Sukarno's policy of *konfrontasi* ("confrontation") against Malaysia, to which Singapore then belonged, but the sentence was carried out after Singapore became independent and after President Suharto had come to power. He interceded on the marines' behalf.

In spite of Indonesia's undoubted importance as a neighbour and of the change of regime that had taken place, Singapore carried out the sentence.

The result was an outbreak of violence in Indonesia that included the sacking of Singapore's Embassy. It took that in its stride, as it did the general downturn in relations with Indonesia which lasted till 1973 when, in a symbolic gesture, Mr Lee Kuan Yew sprinkled flowers on the graves of the marines during his visit to Jakarta. Former Ambassador to Indonesia Lee Khoon Choy, who was instrumental in bringing about the reconciliation, tells the story very well in his *Diplomacy of a Tiny State*.*

The Indonesian position was that the marines had merely been carrying out orders, that those orders had

---

* Second Edition, World Scientific, Singapore, New Jersey, London and Hong Kong, 1993.

been issued during *konfrontasi,* and that the men had not intended to kill anyone. An Indonesian statement spoke of a "similar" case in Malaysia in which 13 men, all Malaysians, had been given the death penalty under the Internal Security Act for associating with armed Indonesians. Following an intervention by Malaysian Prime Minister Tunku Abdul Rahman, the rulers had commuted the sentences to life imprisonment. What Indonesia was seeking for the marines was not freedom but commutation of the death sentences to life imprisonment.

Singapore responded that it had always shown understanding and sympathy for the position of the Indonesian government in dealing with problems arising from the policy of "confrontation" pursued by the previous government. It had thus viewed compassionately cases involving Indonesian nationals who had committed various offences during the "confrontation" where there had been no loss of life. (In a previous case, 43 Indonesian nationals had been released in 1966. Also, in May 1967, two Indonesians, sentenced to death for bringing in a time-bomb which had exploded without causing fatalities, had had their sentences remitted by the President, were freed and were returned to Indonesia.) The case of the marines was different because their sabotage had involved the loss of lives. (In the "similar" Malaysian case cited, there had been no loss of life.)

The point that the marines did not intend to cause casualties was difficult to accept because the bomb had been planted in a crowded building. As for granting a reprieve, Mr Rajaratnam said that setting a precedent by doing so "would have led to a great many difficulties later on". Commentators note that in the Malaysian case, one of the criminals appealing for mercy cited an earlier case in which a female communist's death sentence had been commuted following a clemency campaign. If Singapore granted a reprieve, the chances of future appeals based on it could go on indefinitely. What was there to prevent that?

The Indonesians had asked for clemency or at least a stay of execution. On the latter point, a stay would have benefited the marines only if they had had some hope of a reprieve. That not being the case, the executions were carried out.

"We did what we had to do," Mr Rajaratnam said. "Had we been in Indonesia's place in this issue, we would have taken a similar stand to the one she had taken in doing all she could to save the two men." Similarly, he added, Indonesia should understand Singapore's position.

It is important to keep these details in mind when comparing the case of the marines with that of Fay.

The bombing had caused deaths; Fay's actions had not.

Also, during the crisis over the marines, Singapore was still a young state, indeed, an infant one. Its sovereignty, though acknowledged through its membership of the United Nations, was not yet established incontrovertibly on the ground. To have moved back from carrying out a judgment of its courts could, in those times, have been tantamount to confessing to a sense of insecurity over its sovereignty.

Domestically, if Singapore were to give way over two foreigners because of foreign pressure, what credence could its legal system have had to its own citizens? This was an especially pertinent question since a powerful communist movement was claiming that Singapore, and by implication its legal system, was nothing more than an imperial creation left behind by the British to thwart the people's aspirations.

By contrast, both the Fay affair and Singapore's situation today are very different. Notwithstanding his portrayal in parts of the US media, Fay was not a political issue between the governments of Singapore and the US. No doubt, his government interceded on his behalf, as once the Indonesian government had done over the marines, but the circumstances were different. So was Singapore's international standing. Unlike the ramifications of its decisions two decades ago, the international community would not view a decision to reduce the number of strokes on Fay as anything less than a decision taken by a sovereign nation. The question of *de facto* sovereignty, then hanging in the balance, was now established. Singapore's independence was now acknowledged widely enough for the government's decision, whichever way it went, to be seen as an exercise in sovereignty, not something that raised doubts about its sovereignty.

***

The government's stand on issues it sees as impinging on Singapore's sovereignty was reiterated over a very different kind of issue in 1988. On 7 May that year, it protested to the US over the behaviour of a diplomat whom it accused of involvement in domestic politics. According to a government statement, E. Mason "Hank" Hendrickson, the First Secretary (Political) at the US Embassy, had encouraged several lawyers to stand against the PAP in the next general election (which was held in August 1988). Singapore requested that he be withdrawn — the diplomatic equivalent of saying that he had 48 hours in which to leave.

That was a drastic measure, especially since it had to do with a representative of a friendly country, indeed, a crucial economic and security partner. What could have made it necessary?

It was the nature of his actions, which the statement described in detail.

Diplomats in Singapore were free to meet anyone they pleased, it said. "It is perfectly legitimate for Hendrickson to keep in touch with leaders of the constitutional opposition, as he has done with Chiam See Tong and J.B. Jeyaretnam, in order to analyze and understand Singapore politics."

However, he had also cultivated people who were not politicians but were known to be anti-government, and not only to solicit their views on political issues in Singapore. "Hendrickson had no business to arrange meetings with disaffected lawyers in order to attack the

Singapore Government, and instigate them to stand for elections against the Government."

The statement noted that the government valued Singapore's ties with the US, "a good friend". It believed that the US also valued its relationship with Singapore. It hoped, in this context, that the Administration did not support or condone the diplomat's actions in any way.

But here was the bottomline. "However, as a sovereign nation, Singapore cannot acquiesce in Hendrickson's continuing interference in Singapore's domestic politics. It is disturbing and dismaying that US diplomats have seen fit to act as if they were the colonial power and Singapore their protectorate."

The choice of the word "protectorate" was significant in a statement which, as *The Straits Times* noted, was couched in correct and restrained language. It underlined a fundamental and recurrent concern with Singapore's sovereignty and survival as an independent state.

On 11 May 1988, Mr Wong Kan Seng, who was then Acting Foreign Minister, said that no one in Singapore was arrested for simply opposing the government, but he would be arrested if he conspired with Marxists or communists or became a proxy of foreign interests. Unlike the US, which was large and rich, Singapore had no margin for error. "A bad government will not be just an amusing target for newspaper columnists or a passing phase in our history. It could mean the end of our history as an independent nation."

Mr Lee Kuan Yew said on 1 June 1988 that experience had shown old guard leaders like himself that Washington was an ally of vital security and strategic importance to Singapore. Longer-term interests had therefore been taken into consideration in the response to the Hendrickson affair. Singapore, he said, had been able to protest over the affair because it could still make independent decisions and, unlike US client-states, had not become dependent militarily, politically and economically on US grants and aid.

Ministers spoke to grassroots leaders about foreign interference in Singapore's domestic politics. They said that the affair was a reminder of the Republic's vulnerability. If such attempts succeeded, the consequences could be horrendous, they warned. Singapore's future was for Singaporeans alone to decide; foreigners could not be allowed to interfere. Grassroots leaders agreed, with many expressing anger and disappointment that the US, said to be a friendly country, was actually trying to destabilize Singapore.

Reacting to news that Washington would not reprimand its officials involved because, in the words of a State Department official, "we reject the allegation", several MPs expressed dismay, and some were disappointed over Singapore's response. Dr Lau Teik Soon said that the "strictest action" should be taken to see that intervention did not recur. Mr S. Chandra Das went farther in arguing that he personally thought that the government had been too soft. "Rather than ask the American government to withdraw him, we should expel him. His actions justify an expulsion," he said. Mr Abdullah Tarmugi, who found the US statement "waffling", asked what business it was of a foreign country to collect a group of people and instigate them against the government.

Those responses underline the government's emphasis on sovereignty. By contrast, the Fay affair did not touch on the issue of sovereignty. His supporters focused on the severity of his punishment and his alleged ill-treatment by the police. Unlike the diplomat's actions, which the US government never apologized for publicly, no one said that Fay had a legitimate right to do what he pleaded guilty in court to having done.

What these comparisons point to is that, in deciding to reduce Fay's sentence, Singapore was not acting in an inconsistent manner. The marines, the diplomat and the teenager belong to different orders; in responding to each, different sets of factors came into play.

CHAPTER VI
CONCLUSION

LET US DRAW the strands together. Notwithstanding impressions of a great divide between the West and the East, mainstream public opinion in the US and Singapore was conservative over the Fay issue. In spite of that congruence, however, the US media tried to turn the teenager into a human-rights victim and a symbol of American vulnerability in an age of change; the Singapore media responded by criticizing that stance. The US Administration, noting its media's stance, took a public position on the affair; the Singapore government responded. Both sides had to keep in mind the range and depth of their bilateral relations; those were the parameters within which actions and responses would have to be framed. Singapore reduced Fay's sentence; Washington was disappointed that it had not been commuted, but relations moved forward nevertheless.

The issue is a reminder to Singapore of the challenge a small state faces in trying to uphold its domestic system in an unequal world. If anything, the challenge will grow as the disappearance of the bipolar world reveals the ideological differences within the free world that Cold War solidarities had papered over. This is already apparent in the renewed interna-

Conclusion

tional attention to human rights, which is driven largely by Western interest — whether out of genuine concern, or as part of a political agenda, or both. Differences over the principles and practice of human rights may well become a new source of ideological contention pitting an economically resurgent Asia, in particular, against the West.

Singapore will have to respond to those changes. The important thing is that it continues to do so with its sovereignty intact.

EPILOGUE

MICHAEL FAY appeared on CNN's "Larry King Live" show at the end of June 1994 after his release from prison. To watch him was to see a polite and soft-spoken young man very different from what vicarious media solidarity had turned him into: an American caught on the wrong side of the civilizational divide, a folk-hero elevated to victimhood.

Fay spoke about his punishment with disarming and revealing calm. It was disarming because he disavowed anger and revenge. It was revealing because it refocused attention on his media supporters.

To watch him was to be reminded how much the Fay issue — as distinct from the Fay case — had been a media creation, produced, packaged and delivered with the American media's undeniable virtuosity.

But what was significant was that, after his return to the US, there was hardly any attempt to get him to corroborate what had been said about Fay-beating Singapore. The columnists and commentators who had written about him had moved on to other issues.

In its own way, this was worrying. Using the Fay issue as a marker, many columnists had "mapped" Singapore as politically alien, if not hostile, terrain. To the extent that commentary influences memory, would many Americans remember Singapore in terms of that caricature?

Epilogue

Hopefully, time will transform the passions of the moment into a steady and lasting recognition of the truth.

ABOUT THE AUTHOR

Asad Latif, a Senior Leader/Feature Writer with *The Straits Times,* has been in journalism for 15 years. He was formerly Foreign Editor of *Business Times.*

He received a Master of Letters degree at Cambridge University in 1993. His thesis was on the security of new states.

He is married with a son.